Springboard ▽

student book

1

Jack C. Richards

Oxford University Press

Oxford University Press
198 Madison Avenue, New York, NY 10016 USA
Great Clarendon Street, Oxford OX2 6DP England

Oxford New York
Athens Auckland Bangkok Bogotá Bombay
Buenos Aires Calcutta Cape Town Dar es Salaam
Delhi Florence Hong Kong Istanbul Karachi
Kuala Lampur Madras Madrid Melbourne
Mexico City Nairobi Paris Singapore
Taipei Tokyo Toronto

and associated companies in *Berlin Ibadan*

OXFORD is a trademark of Oxford University Press

Library of Congress Cataloging-in-Publication Data

Richards, Jack C.
     Springboard : student book / Jack C. Richards
          p.   cm.
     ISBN 0-19-435350-8
     1. English language – – Textbooks for foreign speakers.
     2. English language – – Spoken English – – Problems,
     exercises, etc. 3. Listening – – Problems, exercises, etc.
     I. Title.
     PE1128.R465   1997
     428.3 ' 4 – – dc21   97-11076
                                                           CIP

Copyright © 1998 Oxford University Press

Editorial Manager: Chris Foley
Developmental Editor: Karen Brock
Contributing Editor: Paul Riley
Production Editor: Kathleen Sands Boehmer
Editorial Assistant: Ruthanne Crowley
Designer: Susan Brorein
Picture Researcher: Clare Maxwell
Production Manager: Abram Hall
Production and Prepress Services: PC&F, Inc.
Cover design: Keithley Associates Incorporated

Printing (last digit) 10 9 8 7 6 5 4 3 2 1

Printed in Hong Kong

Acknowledgments

Illustrations and realia by: Eliot Bergman, Annie Bissett, Jim
DeLapine, Scott MacNeil, Karen Minot, Rob Schuster, Jeff
Seaver, Nina Wallace

Location and studio photography by: Rick Ashley

Unchained Melody by Hy Zaret and Alex North © 1945 Frank
Music Corp., © Renewed 1983 Frank Music Corp. All Right
Reserved. Used by Permission.

*The publishers would like to thank the following for their permission to
reproduce photographs:* Amy Sancetta/AP-Wide World Photos;
Rob Nelson and Scott Rutherford/Black Star; Comstock;
Mitchell Geber/Corbis-LGI Collection; Johan Elbers, Everett
Collection; Ron Chapple, Jim Cummins, Eugene Gebhardt,
L. Kaltman, and Rob Lang/FPG; Robert Harding Picture Library;
Robert Holmes; Courtesy of the Hyatt Regency; John P. Kelley
and Romilly, Lockyer/The Image Bank; Loren Santan/Impact
Visuals; Robert Brown, James Davis, Mikwako Ikeda, Chuck
Mason, and Jay Thomas/International Stock; Wolfgang Kaehler;
Dimension Films and New Line Cinema/The Kobal Collection;
Anderson/Liaison International; Movie Still Archives; Disney,
David Stoecklein, and Richard Foreman/MPTV Photo Archive;
Lester Glasner Archives, Paramount Pictures/Neal Peters
Collection; Gary O'Conner and David Young-Wolff/Photo Edit;
D.R. and T.L. Schrichte/Photo Resource Hawaii; Jack
Foley/Positive Images; Dan Helms, Rob Tringali, Jr./Sportschrome
USA; All Action, J. Henry Fair/Retna Ltd.; Scott
Harrison/Shooting Star; Star File Photos; Rob Crandall, John
Elk, and Robert Fried/Stock Boston; David Ball, Ed Bock,
Michelle Burgess, Randy Duchaine, Murilo Dutra, John Henley,
Henley & Savage, M. Mastrorillo, Tomas Muscionico/Contact;
John Pelaez, Alon Reininger/Contact, Nancy Santullo, Chuck
Savage, Ford Smith, and Ken Straiton; Wayne Eostep, David H.
Stewart, and David Young Wolff/Tony Stone Images; Barnard
Annebicque, Memory Shop, A. Peristein, A. Tannenbaum, and
Pascal Della Zuaha/Sygma; Jack Vartoogian, and Ulrike Welsch.

CONTENTS

SCOPE AND SEQUENCE

INTRODUCTION

Springboard Student Book 1 is the first in a two-level topic-based conversation and listening course for adult and young adult students at the pre-intermediate to intermediate level. It is organized around high-interest topics that encourage students to talk about what they are most interested in: their own lives, aspirations and interests.

Each topic in *Springboard* is explored from two perspectives and introduced by photographs or artwork that activate students' previous language knowledge and real-world experience. Short interactive tasks and personal surveys guide students toward conversational fluency and help them develop communication skills that can be put to immediate use in real-world situations. The listening component reinforces these skills as students develop listening strategies such as listening for gist, attitude and inference. A variety of international accents are a feature of the recorded dialogues so that students are exposed to English spoken as they may actually encounter it outside the classroom.

The topic-based syllabus of the book was shaped by the topics selected from student surveys. The principle underlying each unit is that students are motivated to talk about topics most closely connected to their lives. In addition, the language they need to discuss such topics should flow naturally from the topics themselves. For this reason, the language models, key expressions and vocabulary in *Springboard* are chosen for their usefulness in giving students clear guidance in developing conversational skills they need to discuss topics of importance to them.

The Project File further encourages students' personal involvement and responsibility for their own learning. This file of learner-centered projects provides students with the opportunity for creativity and personal expression as they interact to perform such projects as creating a dream trip poster and presenting a screenplay. As students plan, carry out and share their projects with classmates, they are given the opportunity to bridge the gap between language study and language use.

UNIT STRUCTURE

Springboard contains 12 four-page units. Each unit is divided into 2 two-page lessons that are organized around a topic or theme. Each lesson opens with photographs or artwork which lead students into the topic of the lesson. Students are then given guided practice in the language and expressions they need to discuss each topic. A listening task provides further modeling and practice, and a culminating activity allows personalization of the topic through a communicative task. Each unit offers a variety of exercises and opportunities for pair and group work.

PROJECT FILE

The Project File follows unit twelve of *Springboard*. Twelve projects, one for each unit of the book, provide students with opportunities to extend the skills they have learned in each unit. Each project is accompanied with directions to students on how to plan, carry out and share their finished work with classmates. Suggestions for using projects to help students build a portfolio, a collection of completed work, is contained in the Teacher's Book. Additional suggestions for portfolio assessment, an evaluation of students' effort and work on the projects, is also contained in the Teacher's Book

GLOSSARY

The *Springboard* Glossary, included in the back of the book, facilitates vocabulary development by including definitions in English of key vocabulary from the units. The concise definitions help focus students on learning vocabulary in context; therefore, definitions reflect the meaning of a word or phrase only as it is used in the units. A pronunciation key and examples of many of the words in context are also included. Photocopiable activities in the Teacher's Book provide further practice of the vocabulary in the Glossary and provide independent learning opportunities for students.

TEACHER'S BOOK

The *Springboard* Teacher's Book provides comprehensive suggestions for the most effective ways of presenting and exploiting the activities in the Student Book. In addition, a variety of options are often suggested with additional follow-up activities. The step-by-step notes provide both novice and experienced teachers practical guidance for classroom teaching. The Teacher's Book also offers suggestions for working with large and mixed ability classes and on how best to exploit the Project File and Glossary. Both levels of the *Springboard* Teacher's Books contain the following features:

- Step-by step instructions for each activity
- Language, pronunciation, teaching and culture notes
- Photocopiable vocabulary development worksheets
- A photocopiable testing program
- Recommendations for assessment using project portfolios
- Photocopiable tapescripts for the audio program
- Answer keys to the Student Book

Thank you to the teachers and students who provided valuable input in the development of *Springboard*:

Brian Asbjornson	Marion Friebus	Robert Hickling	Tina Rowe
Eleanor Barnes	Jeff Fryckman	Charles Horne	Peggy Rule
Rory Baskin	Chisato Furuya	Joanne Johnson	Lynn Shanahan
Adrian Chandler	Rodney Gillett	Haruko Katsura	Wilson Strand
Sandy Clark	Peter Gray	Barbara Kerr	David Woodfield
Sue Collins	William Green	Mia Kim	Junko Yamanaka
Steve Cornwall	Timothy Grose	Amy McNeese	Jane Yang
Robert Dickey	Michael Guest	Terry O'Brien	Sonia Yoshitake
Ron Doughty	Ann Marie Hadzima	Cynthia Omoto	
Daniel Dunkley	Lori Haga	Jack Perkins	
David Clay Dycus	Neil Hargreaves	Carol Rinnert	

I would also like to mention my appreciation of the ongoing reviews of the manuscript by David Dykes and Nick Lambert as well as the editorial feedback of Ellen Shaw and Tab Hamlin.

Finally, I would like to thank the publishing team at Oxford University Press— Karen Brock, Susan Brorein, Bev Curran, Chris Foley, Steven Maginn, Paul Riley, and Kathy Sands Boehmer—who set the highest standards for ESL publishing and whose editorial suggestions and encouragement made the writing of this book a special pleasure. Special thanks also to the Oxford University Press staff in Japan, Korea and Taiwan.

Jack C. Richards
Auckland, New Zealand

GETTING STARTED

► **FAMOUS FRIENDS**

A. PAIR WORK. Listen to famous friends greeting each other. Write the number of the conversation next to the *greeting*, *question*, and *response* you hear.

Greetings	Questions	Responses
_1_ Hello.	____ How are you?	____ Great.
____ Hi.	_1_ How are things?	____ Oh, pretty good.
____ Howdy!	____ How's everything?	____ Fine, thank you.
____ Hey there!	____ How have you been?	_1_ Not bad.
____ Good morning.	____ How's it going?	____ Just fine.
____ Good evening.	____ What's up?	____ Not much.

B. Listen again and check your answers.

C. GROUP WORK. Practice greeting your teacher and your classmates. Use the expressions above.

► LISTENING 📼

A. Listen to how we open and close conversations.

Opening	**Closing**
Good to see you.	Well, talk to you later.
How have you been?	See you later.
How are things?	Have a nice day.

B. Listen to people opening and closing conversations. Write the number of each dialogue next to either *Opening* or *Closing*.

Opening: ☐   ☐   ☐   ☐   **Closing:** ☑   ☐   ☐   ☐

► MAKING FRIENDS

CLASS ACTIVITY. Ask your classmates the questions below. If a classmate answers "yes," write his or her name in the box.

Find someone who...	**Questions**
is wearing designer clothes.	Are you *wearing designer clothes?*
has a driver's license.	Do you *have a driver's license?*
likes pepperoni pizza.	Do you *like pepperoni pizza?*

FIND SOMEONE WHO... ❓

likes to travel abroad		likes reggae music
has two pets		has a part-time job
is a good skier		is easygoing
is named after someone		likes coffee better than tea
likes pepperoni pizza		has a January birthday
has more than 100 CDs		likes action movies
has a younger sister		is a "party animal"
is wearing designer clothes		has blood type O
is athletic		likes to gamble

A. ☐

B. ☐

C. ☑

D. ☐

E. ☐

F. ☐

► MEETING AND GREETING

A. The people above are greeting people they may or may not know. Match the conversations below with a picture.

1. A: Hey, I know you. **B:** No, I don't think so. **A:** My name's John Wolf. **B:** Oh, yes. We met skiing.	**2. A:** Pete! Hi. Remember me? **B:** Mary. Mary Lamb. Oh, yes. I remember you. **A:** Yeah, we met at Bill's party.	**3. A:** Oh, hi. You're Michael, aren't you? **B:** Yes. Michael Crow. **A:** Michael, I'm Emma's sister.
4. A: Hi! Aren't we in the same English class? **B:** Yes, we are. My name's Sue Deer. **A:** Nice to meet you, Sue. I'm George.	**5. A:** Hi. I'm Ann. Ann Fish. **B:** Nice to meet you, Ann. **A:** Nice to meet you too.	**6. A:** Hello. I'm Chris Lion. **B:** Lyon? L-Y-O-N? **A:** No, L-I-O-N.

B. CLASS ACTIVITY. Listen to the conversations. Then walk around the classroom and meet and greet as many class members as you can.

► LISTENING 📼

Listen to people as they meet and discuss names. Write the conversation number next to the kind of name discussed.

First Name ☐   Nickname ☐ *1*   Last Name ☐   Full Name ☐

Kyle — (*Celtic*) "handsome"

Karen — (*Greek*) "pure"

Audrey — (*Teutonic*) "noble, strong"

John (Jack) — (*Hebrew*) "God's precious gift"

Christopher (Chris) — (*Greek*) "Christ-bearer"

Mia — (*Italian*) "mine"

Ruth — (*Hebrew*) "friend or beauty"

Mark — (*Latin*) "hammer"

Sean — (*Irish*) Irish for "John"

Amy — (*Latin*) "beloved"

Naomi — (*Hebrew*) "pleasant"

Kenneth (Ken) — (*Celtic*) "handsome"

Steven (Steve) — (*Greek*) "crown"

Charles (Chuck) — (*Teutonic*) "strong"

Susan (Sue) — (*Hebrew*) "Lily"

Paul — (*Latin*) "small"

► FAVORITE NAMES

A. Rate the common English names below. Check (✔) a box for each name.

		I like this name a lot	This name is OK	I don't like this name
FEMALE	Julia	☐	☐	☐
	Jessica	☐	☐	☐
	Lisa	☐	☐	☐
	Emily	☐	☐	☐
	Sarah	☐	☐	☐
MALE	Christopher	☐	☐	☐
	Bruce	☐	☐	☐
	Kevin	☐	☐	☐
	Michael	☐	☐	☐
	Matthew	☐	☐	☐

B. GROUP WORK. Vote on favorite male and female names and share them with the class.

Questions	Group Reporting
How many voted for the name **Julia**? How many for **Christopher?**	Our favorite names are... Names we think are OK are... Names we don't like are...

A. 4

B.

C.

D.

E.

F.

► TYPES OF MUSIC 🔲

A. What type of music are the musicians above playing? Match each photo with a *type of music* from the list below. There are more types of music than photos.

Types of Music							
1. rock	**2.** rap	**3.** reggae	**4.** jazz	**5.** country	**6.** New Age	**7.** techno	**8.** classical

B. Listen to a person switching radio stations. What types of music do you hear? As you listen number the boxes from the **Types of Music** list.

A. 6   B. ☐   C. ☐   D. ☐   E. ☐   F. ☐   G. ☐   H. ☐

C. PAIR WORK. Talk about types of music you like and dislike. Use the model below.

A: What kind of music do you like?
B: Well, I like **reggae**.
A: Do you like **rap**?
B: *I love it.*

Expressing Likes and Dislikes

I love it.	*Not very much.*	*No, I don't like it.*
I really like it.		*I can't stand it.*

► LISTENING 🔲

A. PAIR WORK. Pre-listening. Can you guess what *type of music* the people below listen to? Write your guess above the pictures.

1. *New Age*	2. _____	3. _____	4. _____

Mr. Hayes	**Kristin**	**Hillary**	**Carl**

1. *rap*	2. _____	3. _____	4. _____

B. Now listen to Mr. Hayes, Kristin, Hillary, and Carl talking about music. Write the kind of music they really like below their names.

► FAVORITES SURVEY

GROUP WORK. Complete the **Favorites Survey**. Then take turns asking and responding to questions about the survey items. Use the model below.

🎵 FAVORITES

① **Female vocalist**	
② **Male vocalist**	
③ **Band**	
④ **Type of music**	
⑤ **Karaoke song to sing**	
⑥ **Dance music**	
⑦ **Place to buy CDs**	
⑧ **Song at the moment**	
⑨ **Childhood song**	
⑩ **Movie or TV soundtrack**	

A: So, who's your favorite **female vocalist**?
B: *That's easy. It's...*
A: And who's your favorite **male vocalist**?
　　　　　　OR
　And what's your favorite **band**?
B: *I really don't have one.*

Responding to Questions
....
That's easy. It's...
Let me think. I guess it's...
It's hard to say, but I guess it's...
I really don't have one.

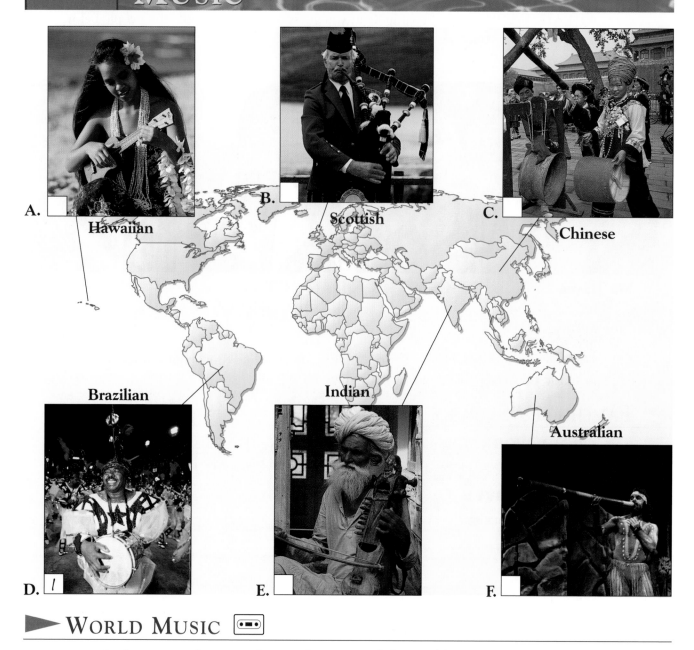

A. Hawaiian
B. Scottish
C. Chinese
Brazilian
Indian
Australian
D. *1*
E.
F.

► WORLD MUSIC 🔘

A. Listen to selections of music from around the world. Number the photos as you listen.

B. GROUP WORK. Listen to the music selections again. How do you like them? Describe your reactions in groups. Use the model below.

A: What do you think of **Scottish** music?	**Adjectives to Describe Music**	
OR	**+**	**−**
How do you like **Hawaiian** music?	beautiful	nothing special
B: It's │ beautiful.	nice	a little strange
│ nothing special.	interesting	boring
How about you?	lively	too loud
Do you like it?	relaxing	horrible
A: Well, it's *interesting*.	easy to listen to	terrible

A. PAIR WORK. Love songs appear in music around the world. Complete the American love song *Unchained Melody* with words from the box.

Unchained Melody

Oh, my _____ , my darling,
    1

I've hungered for your _____ a long lonely _____ .
                          2   3

And time goes by so _____ and time can do so _____ ;
                        4   5

Are you still _____ ? I need your love, I need your _____ ,
                6   7

God speed your love to _____ .
                          8

Lonely rivers flow to the _____ , to the _____ ,
                            9   10

to the open arms of the sea

Lonely rivers sigh, "Wait for _____ , wait for me.
                                11

I'll be coming _____ , wait for me."
                12

home	love	love	me	me	mine
much	sea	sea	slowly	time	touch

B. Now listen to the song and check your answers. Then sing the song.

► MUSIC CRITIC

A. Rank each statement about *Unchained Melody* from 1 (agree) to 5 (disagree). Circle your answers, then total your score in the space provided.

1. I really like *Unchained Melody*.	1	2	3	4	5
2. *Unchained Melody* is a beautiful love song.	1	2	3	4	5
3. The male vocalist's voice is nice.	1	2	3	4	5
4. I want to listen to *Unchained Melody* again.	1	2	3	4	5
5. I would like to give *Unchained Melody* to a friend.	1	2	3	4	5

Total Score _____

B. GROUP WORK. Who liked *Unchained Melody* the most (highest score) and the least (lowest score)? Compare your scores.

C. GROUP WORK. Decide on and list five love songs *everyone* in the group likes. Choose at least one from another part of the world. Present your top five list to the class.

LEARNING FOR LIFE

► WHY STUDY ENGLISH?

A. PAIR WORK. Decide why each of the people above might be learning English. Use the model below.

	Reasons
A: Why do you think she's learning English?	
	to pass an exam. because it's required.
B: I guess *to pass an exam.*	to meet friends. because he likes languages.
OR	to travel abroad. because she wants to...
I don't know. Maybe *to pass an exam.*	to get a better job.
A: Yeah, she's probably studying *because it's required.*	to study overseas.

B. GROUP WORK. Discuss why you are learning English. Then share your information with the class. Use the model below.

Only one Two Three All	of us	is are	studying English	to... because...

A. PAIR WORK. Listen to Tom and Mari, and then Ken and Naomi talking about learning English. Tell your partner why each person is learning English.

B. Listen again and check (✔) the things they do to learn English.

Conversation 1	Tom	Mari
studies grammar	☐	☐
dates an English speaker	☐	☐
uses the Internet	✔	☐
listens to radio	☐	☐
sends e-mail in English	✔	☐

Conversation 2	Ken	Naomi
goes to movies	☐	☐
sings in the shower	☐	☐
practices common expressions	☐	☐
reads magazines	☐	☐
reads comic books	☐	☐

▶ LANGUAGE LEARNING STRATEGIES

A. What strategies do you use to improve your English? Check (✔) the strategies you use and add at least one of your own.

STRATEGIES

☐ 1. I practice speaking English at home.

☐ 2. I practice using common expressions.

☐ 3. I listen to songs in English.

☐ 4. I listen to radio programs in English.

☐ 5. I write down words in a vocabulary book.

☐ 6. I send e-mail messages in English.

☐ 7. I read books in English.

☐ 8. I stop foreigners and ask them questions.

☐ 9. _____

B. GROUP WORK. Talk about strategies you use to improve your English. Then share your information with the class. Use the model below.

> **A:** In our group the top strategies were **listening to songs in English** and...
>
> **B:** Several people
> Some | **practice speaking English at home.**
> Not many
>
> Nobody | **stops foreigners and asks them questions.**

►SCHOOL DAYS

A. What do you think are the most important things you learn at school? Add one more to the list below, then check (✔) the five most important to you.

_____ learning how to get along with people	_____ finding out what you are good at
_____ learning skills you need to get a job	_____ having a good time
_____ learning to think on your own	_____ developing good communication skills
_____ learning to see other points of view	_____ making life-long friends
_____ _____	

B. PAIR WORK. Discuss your views on the important things you learn at school. Use the model below.

A: So, what's important for you?

B: I guess for me
    OR
  Well, I'd have to say | **having a good time**
  But, I'd also say | **learning to think on your own** | is important.
    I also think

A. Sandy, Richard, and Wendy are students at a university. Listen to them discussing their studies. Circle the courses and activities they like most.

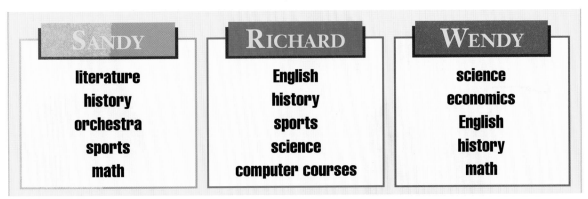

SANDY	RICHARD	WENDY
literature	English	science
history	history	economics
orchestra	sports	English
sports	science	history
math	computer courses	math

B. Now listen to descriptions of courses at their school. Check (✔) who would enjoy the course most.

	Course 1	Course 2	Course 3	Course 4
Sandy				
Richard	✔			
Wendy				

► SCHOOL SURVEY

GROUP WORK. Take turns asking and answering the survey questions.

1. What's the most useful course you've ever taken?
2. What subject have you enjoyed the most?
3. What subjects have you really hated?
4. What's the most difficult course you've taken?
5. Who's the best teacher you've ever had? Why?
6. Is there anything you'd like to change about school?

FASHION

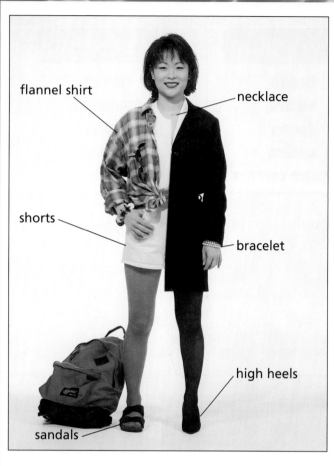

flannel shirt — necklace

shorts

bracelet

high heels

sandals

leather jacket — necktie

suspenders

torn jeans

suit

work boots

▶ WHAT'S IN?

A. PAIR WORK. What's *in* for you and your partner? Talk about which items above you like for guys and girls. Use the model below.

A: What do you think about | **torn jeans?**
    Do you like
B: I think they look *great.*
A: Really? Me too.
        OR
    Really? I think they look *tacky.*

Adjectives to Describe Fashion

+	+/−	−
great	so-so	tacky*
stylish	all right	outdated
cool*	kind of neat*	old-fashioned
attractive	average	sloppy
classy	pretty good	ugly
		informal

B. GROUP WORK. With your partner join another pair of students. Take turns asking and answering questions about personal fashion.

1. What colors do you like to wear most often?
2. What are your three favorite items of clothing?
3. What is something you'd never wear? Why?
4. If you could spend as much money as you like on clothes and accessories, what would you buy?

A. Listen to Diane and Paul talking about the clothes and accessories below. Number the pictures as you listen.

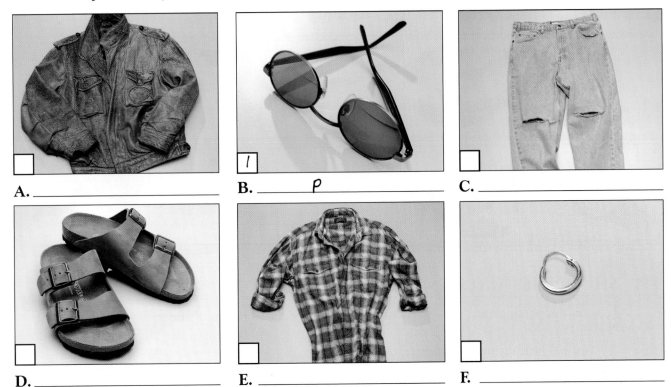

A. _____

B. _____ *P* _____

C. _____

D. _____

E. _____

F. _____

B. Now listen to Diane and Paul talking about items they will wear to a party. Write *D* under the items Diane will wear, and *P* under the items Paul will wear.

▶ PARTY TIME

PARTY TIME!
End of Summer Barbecue

Date: Saturday, August 14th
Time: 6:00 p.m.
Place: Cindy's house
144 Green Street

*Prize for couple with coolest look

You are invited to a dinner party on August 14th at 7 p.m. to welcome Julia Lee, visiting student from Taiwan

Place: Home of Dr. and Mrs. Williamson, 15 Hobden Street

PAIR WORK. You have received invitations to two parties. Decide which party you will attend. Then take turns describing the outfit you will wear. Use the model below.

| A: Since it's a | casual formal | party, I am going to wear | jeans. a suit. |

I'll also wear...
I'm not going to wear...

Price	Comfort	Quality	Brand Name	Look

SHOPPING VALUES

A. How important is *price*, *comfort*, *quality*, the *brand name*, or the *look* when you shop? Fill in the chart for the items below. Put a check (✔) for important shopping values and an (✗) for unimportant ones.

Shopping Values

	Price	Comfort	Quality	Brand Name	Look	

B. PAIR WORK. Discuss what's important and unimportant to you when you buy the clothes and accessories in the chart. Use the model below.

A: What's important for you when you buy a *shirt*?

B: Well, I guess | price / comfort / quality | is the most important thing. / is the next most important thing.

I'm not very concerned about the | brand name. / look.

▶ LISTENING 📼

Listen to Rita, Greg, Eric, and Amy telling a friend about items they bought recently. Write the item they bought and check (✔) which shopping values were important to them.

Name	Item	Shopping Values			
		Price	Look	Brand Name	Quality
1. Rita	shirt	✔	✔		
2. Greg					
3. Eric					
4. Amy					

▶ FASHION COMPLIMENTS

A. PAIR WORK When friends meet they sometimes greet each other by giving a compliment about what they are wearing. With a partner practice the compliments and responses below.

Compliments		Responses
That's a neat shirt.		I got it on sale.
I like your running shoes.		They're really comfortable.
That's a nice looking watch.	Thanks.	It's waterproof, too.
Hey, I love your L.L. Bean boots.		You can't beat L.L. Bean!
I like your new glasses.		My old ones were too old-fashioned.

B. CLASS ACTIVITY. Move around the classroom and greet your classmates. Compliment them on what they are wearing.

GREAT ESCAPES

camping trip
- go mountain climbing
- sleep outdoors
- look at the stars

beach vacation
- go snorkeling
- lie in the sun
- eat lobster

city vacation
- visit night spots
- go shopping
- go to museums

bus tour
- travel in comfort
- travel with a group
- see small towns on the way

safari trip
- watch wild animals
- visit unusual places
- take pictures

your ideal vacation

_____
_____
_____

▶ VACATION ACTIVITIES

A. Look at the activities you can do on the vacations above. Then draw a picture of your ideal vacation and add activities you can do.

B. PAIR WORK. Talk about your favorite vacations and share them with the class.

A: My favorite vacation is a **camping trip**.
B: *That sounds nice.*
A: I like to **sleep outdoors** and **look at the stars**.
B: *Me too.*
A: I also like **beach vacations**. I love to…
B: I | love that | too.
  | do |
	Expressing Interest
	That sounds | nice.
	  | fun.
	Is that right?
	Me too.
	I love that too.
	I do too.

Our favorite vacations are **city vacations** and **bus tours**.
On a **city vacation** we like to go shopping and…

COME TO KAUAI & VACATION HAWAIIAN STYLE

☐ Horseback ride on the beach
☐ Bicycle down a mountain
☐ Snorkel
☐ Take a helicopter ride

☐ Eat Kona lobster
☐ Watch hula dancers
☐ Stay at the Hyatt Regency
☐ Relax and swim at the pool

▶ LISTENING

Listen to Jodie and Simon sharing stories about their vacation to Kauai. Write *J* for Jodie and *S* for Simon in the boxes that describe their activities.

▶ TRAVEL SURVEY

GROUP WORK. Ask each other the travel survey questions and add two more of your own.

1. Where's an unusual place you would like to visit? Why?
2. What do you like to do when you visit a new city?
3. Do you like to travel with a group? Why or why not?
4. Where's an ideal place for a honeymoon?
5. How many days make an ideal vacation?

6. _____

7. _____

SINGAPORE

SINGAPORE ZOO

LITTLE INDIA

RAFFLES HOTEL

ORCHARD ROAD

JURONG BIRD PARK

HAW PAR VILLA DRAGON WORLD

SENTOSA ISLAND

CABLE CAR STATION

CLARKE QUAY

ARAB DISTRICT

CHINATOWN

Woodlands Rd. · Admirality Rd. · Mandai Rd. · Sembawang Rd. · Choa Chu Kang Rd. · Bahar Rd. · Jalan · Upper Bukit Timah Rd. · Commonwealth Ave. · Pan Island Expressway · Bukit Timah Rd. · Ayer Rajah Rd. · Upper Thomson Rd. · Orchard Rd. · Serangoon Rd. · Tampines Expressway · Pan Island Expressway

► **SINGAPORE VACATION**

A. PAIR WORK. Talk about the things you would like to do and not like to do in Singapore. Use the model below.

> **A:** What are some of the things you'd like to do in Singapore?
>
> **B:** Well, I'd like to visit **Jurong Bird Park.** That sounds interesting.
>
> **A:** Yeah, me too. Would you like to take the cable car to **Sentosa Island?**
>
> **B:** That sounds nice.
>   OR
> No, I don't think so.

B. Rank the activities you would like to do from 1 (you like the most) to 5 (you like the least) and compare them with a partner.

Listen to Brian discussing his photos of a recent vacation to Singapore. Number the vacation photos from 1 to 6 as you listen.

A. ☐

B. ☐

C. ☐

D. ☐

E. ☐

F. 1

► AFTERNOON IN SINGAPORE

GROUP WORK. Discuss a plan for an afternoon in Singapore. Use the trolley schedule and model below and the map on page 20. Begin at Orchard Road at 12:00 PM and return there by 6:30 PM. Be sure to allow time to enjoy each place you stop.

THE SINGAPORE TROLLEY

HOURLY SCHEDULE		
TROLLEY STOPS	TROLLEY 1	TROLLEY 2
Orchard Road	:00	:30
Chinatown	:05	:35
Raffles Hotel	:07	:37
Clarke Quay	:10	:40
Cable car to Sentosa	:15	:45
Haw Par Villa Dragon World	:20	:50
Jurong Bird Park	:30	:00
Singapore Zoo	:45	:15

Afternoon Plan

	Place	Time
Leave:	Orchard Road	12:00
Arrive:	Chinatown	12:05
Leave:	Chinatown	1:35
Arrive:	Clarke Quay	1:40

Let's go to **Chinatown** first and have lunch. Let's leave at 1:35 for **Clarke Quay** to shop.

▶ AN IDEAL DATE

A. Check (✔) all the boxes below that describe your ideal date. Add one more word or expression to each list.

♥ DATE PROFILE

TYPE	INTERESTS	LOOKS
☐ athletic	☐ sports	☐ attractive
☐ homebody	☐ music	☐ gorgeous
☐ easygoing	☐ nature	☐ cute
☐ brainy	☐ travel	☐ average-looking
☐ party animal	☐ movies	☐ sexy
☐	☐	☐

B. PAIR WORK. Take turns describing your ideal date. Use the model below.

A: So, what's your ideal date like?

B: Well, I like the *easygoing* type.

My ideal date would be interested in *travel* and *movies*.

A: How about looks?

B: Ideally, | he / she | would be *attractive*.   OR   I don't really care.

Listen to Tina, Paula, Jack, and Adam describing their ideal dates. Match the *type* of person they like to date and that person's *interests*.

	Type	Interests	Type	Interests
1. Tina	*d*	*g*	**a.** easygoing	**e.** dance clubs
2. Paula	_____	_____	**b.** brainy	**f.** going to the beach
3. Jack	_____	_____	**c.** party animal	**g.** music
4. Adam	_____	_____	**d.** homebody	**h.** politics

► SOCIAL LIFE POLL

A. How is your social life? Complete these statements with the words below or ones of your own.

TERRIFIC   **GREAT**   **GOOD**
OK   **TERRIBLE**

1. Right now my social life is _____.

2. Most of my friends are _____.

3. I think going to parties is _____.

4. If I have to spend a Saturday night on my own, I feel _____.

5. In photographs I usually look _____.

6. When I meet someone attractive I feel _____.

7. If I meet someone attractive and they don't talk to me, I feel _____.

8. The last person I dated was _____.

9. The last person I dated probably thought I was _____.

10. When I break up with someone I've been dating I feel _____.

B. PAIR WORK. Discuss the answers to the social life poll. Use the model below.

	Reactions
A: Right now my social life is **terrific**.	*No kidding!*
B: *No kidding!* My social life is...	*Oh, really?*
A: And let's see. **Most of my friends are...**	*Same with me.*
	I know what you mean.

UNIT 6 | DATING

► YOUR DATING STYLE

GROUP WORK. Complete the survey to determine your dating style. Then discuss your styles.

♡ DATING STYLE SURVEY

❶ Do you prefer to date someone your own age, someone older, or younger?
I prefer to date someone *my own age/older/younger*.

❷ Do you think people should "go Dutch"?
I *think/don't think* people should "go Dutch".

❸ Would you ever date your friend's boyfriend or girlfriend?
I'd *date/never date* my friend's _____.

❹ Would you like to date someone from a different culture?
I'd *like/wouldn't like* to date someone from a different culture.

❺ How long does it take you to get ready for a date?
It takes me about _____.

❻ How many dates should a couple go on before they are "going steady"?
- ☐ 1 date
- ☐ 3-5 dates
- ☐ 5-10 dates
- ☐ _____

A couple should go on_____before they are "going steady".

❼ I will break up with someone if he/she _____.
- ☐ has bad manners
- ☐ has no money
- ☐ forgets my birthday
- ☐ gains a lot of weight
- ☐ has another girl/boyfriend
- ☐ smokes
- ☐ doesn't call for two weeks
- ☐ _____

I will break up with someone if he/she _____

❽ Which of the following are unacceptable for someone you are dating?
- ☐ wears glasses
- ☐ is sloppy
- ☐ once dated my best friend
- ☐ works in the same office
- ☐ is much taller than I am
- ☐ is much smaller than I am
- ☐ lives very far away
- ☐ _____

Someone is unacceptable if he/she _____

❾ Which is more important, LOVE or MONEY?
_____ is definitely more important than_____.

❿ Which is more important, LOOKS or SENSE OF HUMOR?
I don't care about_____. _____ is/are more important.

24 • UNIT 6 DATING

Listen to Peggy, Phil, and Jill describing what they like to do on a date. For each conversation number *two* photos.

A.

B.

C. *I*

D.

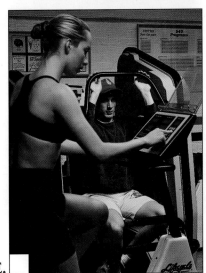

E.

F.

► DREAM DATE

PAIR WORK. Talk about three or four things you would do on a dream date. Add at least one other of your own. Use the model below.

	Choices
A: So, what do you think you'd do?	
B: I guess we'd *go for a drive* in the morning. In the afternoon we'd *go to the movies*. Then we'd *go out to dinner* in the evening. After that we'd probably *go dancing*.	go to — a video arcade / an amusement park / the movies
	go — out to dinner / shopping / dancing
A: That sounds fun. Well, I think my date and I would…	go for a — drive / bike ride

FOOD FOR THOUGHT

90 or 190   100 or 150
100 or 200
350 or 560
220 or 370
140 or 250
190 or 240
50 or 100
300 or 400
175 or 275
175 or 225
100 or 200

► SNACKS

A. PAIR WORK. Do you ever think about the food you eat? Some popular food and snacks are pictured above. Guess the correct calorie counts. Use the model below.

> **A:** How many calories do you think there are in a **glass of orange juice?**
> **B:** In a **glass of orange juice?** I'd say *100*.
> **A:** Really? I think it's more. I'd say *200*.
>   OR
>   Yes, I think you're right. OK. The next one. How many...

B. Now listen and circle the correct information.

C. GROUP WORK. Take turns asking and answering the survey questions below.

1. What are your two favorite snacks?
2. What is your favorite convenience store for buying a snack?
3. How much money do you spend a day on snacks?
4. Do you prefer sweet snacks or salty snacks?
5. Which snack from the photo above would you like right now?

Listen to Allen, Linda, Karen, and Tim talking about their favorite foods. Circle the favorite food they describe.

FAVORITE FOOD

Allen			
Linda			
Karen			
Tim			

► FOOD AROUND TOWN

A. What are your favorite foods and restaurants? Complete the **Favorites** chart below.

FAVORITES

Hot drink _____

Fruit juice _____

Home-cooked dinner _____

Dessert _____

Pizza topping _____

Flavor of ice cream _____

Food from another country _____

Family restaurant _____

Fast-food restaurant _____

Coffee shop _____

B. GROUP WORK. Ask and respond to questions about favorite foods and restaurants around town. Use the model below.

A: What's your favorite **hot drink?**

B: Hmmm. Let's see. *I guess my favorite is* Earl Grey tea.

OR

I don't really have a favorite. I like both coffee and tea.

OR

Well, it depends. In the morning I like coffee, but...

Expressing Favorites

I guess my favorite is...

I don't really have a favorite.

Well, it depends.

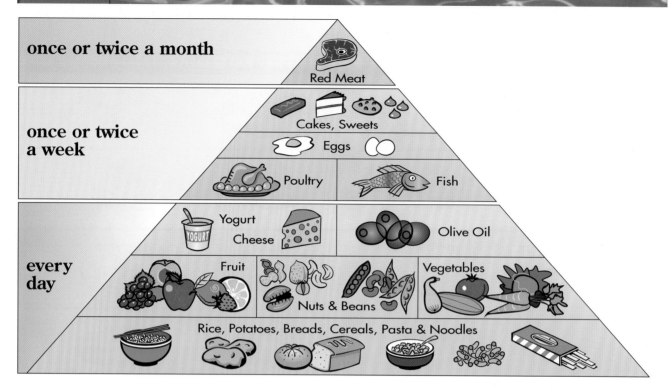

once or twice a month

once or twice
a week

every
day

Red Meat

Cakes, Sweets

Eggs

Poultry   Fish

Yogurt
Cheese   Olive Oil

Fruit   Vegetables

Nuts & Beans

Rice, Potatoes, Breads, Cereals, Pasta & Noodles

► THE MEDITERRANEAN DIET

Did you know that people in the Mediterranean region have long life spans and little heart disease? Look at the food pyramid of their typical diet above.

A. PAIR WORK. Talk about foods from the pyramid and other foods you eat. Use the model below.

A: I love cake.
B: Me too. I *always* eat it.
        OR
   Not me. I *hardly ever* eat it.
A: I eat it *all the time*.

Frequency Expressions		
always		hardly ever
sometimes		never
daily		
once in a while	twice	week
all the time	three times	a month

B. In the chart below list as many foods as you can in your diet.

✓ MY DIET

DAILY	ONCE OR TWICE A WEEK	ONCE OR TWICE A MONTH

C. Now on a separate sheet of paper, draw *your* food pyramid. Is it similar to or different from your partner's?

Listen to people who have lived in Thailand, Italy, and Egypt describing the diet of those countries. Check (✔) the foods they *eat often* and leave an empty box for foods they *eat less often*.

1. Thailand	2. Italy	3. Egypt
✔ curries	☐ pasta	☐ rice
☐ beef	☐ cheese	☐ bread
☐ chicken	☐ salads	☐ potatoes
☐ pork	☐ chicken	☐ lamb
☐ turkey	☐ beef	☐ chicken
☐ lamb	☐ veal	☐ pork
☐ bread	☐ tea	☐ tea
☐ rice	☐ coffee	☐ coffee

► CLASS DINNER PARTY

A. GROUP WORK. Your class is having a class dinner party this weekend. Plan a meal together and then fill in the menu below.

Class Dinner Party

~ *Menu* ~

Appetizer:

Main Course:

Dessert:

Drinks:

B. Report your group's menu to the class. Vote for the best menu. You may vote for your own!

PERSONALITIES

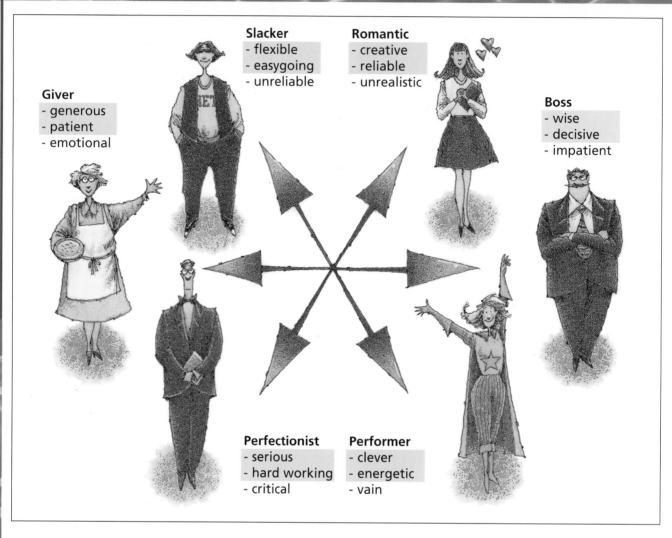

Giver
- generous
- patient
- emotional

Slacker
- flexible
- easygoing
- unreliable

Romantic
- creative
- reliable
- unrealistic

Boss
- wise
- decisive
- impatient

Perfectionist
- serious
- hard working
- critical

Performer
- clever
- energetic
- vain

▶ PERSONALITY TYPES

A. PAIR WORK. Look at the personality types on the chart above. Then take turns talking about your personality type. Use the model below.

	Asking for Examples
A: How would you describe yourself?	*Really? Why do you say that?*
B: I think I'm part / I'm a bit of a **slacker** and part / but more of a **romantic.**	*Really? Can you give me an example?*
A: *Really? Why do you say that?*	
B: Well, I'm very **easygoing,** but I am **reliable.** For example, I…	

B. GROUP WORK. With your partner join another pair and find out their personality types. Discuss personality types in your group and report to the class.

In our group we have two **slackers**, one **boss**, and…

Bruce

Hannah

Sam

David

Listen to people talking about Bruce, Hannah, Sam, and David. Check (✔) the best word to describe each person.

1. ✔ generous	**2.** ☐ serious	**3.** ☐ patient	**4.** ☐ critical
☐ clever	☐ emotional	☐ reliable	☐ energetic
☐ impatient	☐ easygoing	☐ decisive	☐ creative

► Personality Traits

PAIR WORK. With your partner decide and write the *two* most important personality traits for the people in the chart. Use the model below.

A: What personality traits should a **teacher** have?

B: A **teacher?** Well, a **teacher** | should ought to | be | *patient.* What do you think?

A: Yes, *patient* and *wise.*

B: How about *energetic?*

A: Yes, but *patient* and *wise* are the most important.

B: Yes, I agree.
          OR
I don't know. I think *patient* and *energetic* are the most important.

1. Teacher	2. Parent	3. Best Friend	4. Son or Daughter
_____	_____	_____	_____
_____	_____	_____	_____

► THE BEST AND WORST

A. Look at statements people make about themselves. Check (✔) the ones that are true about you.

1. ☐ I daydream a lot.
2. ☐ I often talk to myself.
3. ☐ I'm patient.
4. ☐ I like things perfect.
5. ☐ I'm always on time.
6. ☐ I get frustrated easily.
7. ☐ I have a good sense of humor.
8. ☐ I fall in love very easily.
9. ☐ I'm very emotional.
10. ☐ I waste a lot of time.

11. ☐ I'm a good listener.
12. ☐ I'm creative.
13. ☐ I get along well with people.
14. ☐ I worry too much about my looks.
15. ☐ I always keep my word.
16. ☐ I get stressed out easily.
17. ☐ I cry easily.
18. ☐ I'm very well-organized.
19. ☐ I often lose my temper.
20. ☐ I'm too lazy to exercise.

B. PAIR WORK. Use the statements you checked above to describe your best and worst traits to your partner. Use the model below.

A: One of my worst traits is **I waste a lot of time.**
B: Really? Is that right?
A: Yes, when I get home from school, I sit and read magazines for hours.

▶ LISTENING 📼

A. Listen to people talking about their friends. In the picture above number the person described in each conversation.

B. Listen again. Do the people describe something positive or something negative about their friends? Check (✔) positive or negative below.

	1. Ted	**2.** Jenny	**3.** Doug	**4.** Rose	**5.** Bob	**6.** Julia
Positive	☐	☐	☐	☐	☐	☐
Negative	✔	☐	☐	☐	☐	☐

▶ PERSONALITY SURVEY

PAIR WORK. Ask each other these questions.

1. Do you ever talk to yourself? When? Aloud or silently?
2. Do you sometimes get stressed out? When? What do you do to relax?
3. What would you change about yourself if you could?
4. What kind of people do you get along well with?
5. What kind of people do you not get along well with?
6. What's your best friend like? How similar is he or she to you?

CAREER DREAMS

A.

B.

C.

D.

E.

F. *1*

► PART-TIME JOBS

A. Most people's first experience with the world of work is a part-time job. Match each job below with the correct photo and add two more part-time jobs to the list.

1. working in an information booth
2. handing out flyers
3. working as a tour guide
4. delivering pizzas
5. working at a fast-food restaurant
6. selling newspaper subscriptions
7. _____
8. _____

B. PAIR WORK. What do you think of these part-time jobs? Discuss the ones from the list above. Use the model below.

A: What do you think of **delivering pizzas**?
B: It sounds *easy* to me.
A: Yeah, and I guess it's *fun* at times.
         OR
   Maybe, but I bet it's *boring* at times too.

Adjectives to Describe Jobs

+	−
easy	boring
fun	tiring
exciting	exhausting
interesting	stressful
challenging	difficult

A. Listen to Carol, Jim, John, and Kathy talking about their part-time jobs. Write the number of the job they describe from the list of jobs on page 34.

1. Carol _____4_____   2. Jim _____   3. John _____   4. Kathy _____

B. Now listen to the rest of the conversation. Circle the correct answers.

	Job Satisfaction	Reason	Job Qualities
1. Carol	☺ ☹	⟨easy⟩ difficult	⟨energetic⟩ flexible
2. Jim	☺ ☹	easy tiring	persuasive patient
3. John	☺ ☹	interesting boring	good communicator persuasive
4. Kathy	☺ ☹	exciting boring	patient flexible

▶ JOB REQUIREMENTS

Tutor

Model

Ski Instructor

A. PAIR WORK. What are two important qualities you need for the part-time jobs in the photos above? With your partner discuss the jobs of *tutor*, *model*, and *ski instructor*.

A: I guess for a **tutor** you need to be *a good listener*.
B: Yes, and you also have to be *flexible*.
A: Do you think you need to be *persuasive*?
B: No, I don't think that's so important.
          OR
   Yes, I think that's very important.

Job Qualities

a good listener	*patient*
a good communicator	*persuasive*
a quick thinker	*energetic*
	flexible

B. What job qualities do you have? Take turns describing a part-time job that suits your qualities.

Well, I'm a *good communicator* and I'm *patient,* so I think I'd be a good **tutor.**

Job Satisfaction

Salary

Travel Opportunities

Job Security

Company Reputation

Working Hours

Benefits

► JOB FACTORS

A. PAIR WORK. What factors are important to you in a career? Choose the two most important factors and compare with your partner.

> A: For me the most important factors are **salary** and **benefits**.
> B: Don't you think **job satisfaction** is an important factor?
> A: Maybe, but less important than the others.
> B: My top two job factors are **working hours** and **job security**.

B. GROUP WORK. Take turns asking and answering these questions.

> A: Would you prefer to work in an office or outdoors?
> B: I'd prefer to work outdoors if possible. I think office work is boring.

1. Would you prefer to work in an office or outdoors?
2. Would you rather work for a male or female boss?
3. Would you prefer to work for someone else or be self-employed?
4. Would you rather have a secure job with a lower salary, or a job with less security but a higher salary?
5. Would you rather have a career in the arts or in business?

► LISTENING 📼

Listen to Rod, Corinna, Kurt, and Liz talking about their jobs. Circle the two most important factors for them in choosing their jobs.

1. Rod	working hours	(job security)	salary	(job satisfaction)
2. Corinna	company reputation	job security	salary	benefits
3. Kurt	job satisfaction	working hours	salary	travel opportunities
4. Liz	company reputation	job security	salary	travel opportunities

► CHOOSE YOUR JOB

A. Which job would you like to have? From the list of jobs below check (✔) the job or jobs you'd like to have. Add one of your own.

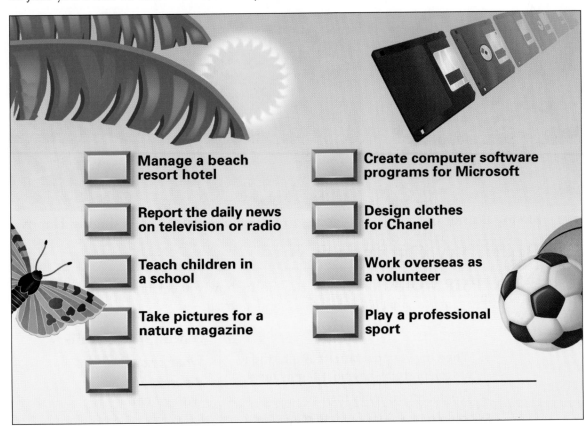

☐ **Manage a beach resort hotel**

☐ **Report the daily news on television or radio**

☐ **Teach children in a school**

☐ **Take pictures for a nature magazine**

☐ _____

☐ **Create computer software programs for Microsoft**

☐ **Design clothes for Chanel**

☐ **Work overseas as a volunteer**

☐ **Play a professional sport**

B. PAIR WORK. Take turns discussing which jobs appeal to you and why. Use the model below.

> **A:** I would really like to **design clothes for Chanel.**
> **B:** Really? What appeals to you about that job?
> **A:** Well, **company reputation** and **salary.** The other factors are not very important.

CUSTOMS

having a family meal

arranging a surprise party

going on a trip

having dinner out

going to a special event

singing Happy Birthday

► BIRTHDAY CELEBRATIONS

A. PAIR WORK. Take turns explaining how you celebrate birthdays for *brothers and sisters, parents, grandparents, friends,* and *yourself.*

A: When my younger sister has a birthday, we celebrate by **having a family meal.**
B: *What kind* of family meal?
A: Usually my sister's favorite meal.

Asking for Details

What kind?

Where?

With whom?

B. GROUP WORK. Take turns talking about birthdays.
1. When is your birthday?
2. Which was your first birthday you remember?
3. Which birthday was the most memorable?
4. What is the most unusual birthday gift you have ever received?
5. What is the best birthday gift you have given to someone?
6. What would you like to do on your next birthday?

Listen to friends deciding on birthday gifts. Match each person with his or her gift. Listen again and match the reason for the gift.

	Gift	Reason
1. Lisa's father	plant	something the person likes
	money	something different
2. Miss Gibson	book	something the person needs
	CD	something personal
3. Cindy	chocolates	not expected
	picture	
	movie tickets	
4. Kyle	necktie	

► BIRTHDAY GIFTS

GROUP WORK. Check (✔) which gifts would be acceptable for the people listed. Then discuss your choices. Use the model below.

GIFTS

	Brother/Sister	Boyfriend/Girlfriend	Mother	Father	Boss/Teacher
Money	☐	☐	☐	☐	☐
Chocolate	☐	☐	☐	☐	☐
A CD	☐	☐	☐	☐	☐
A book	☐	☐	☐	☐	☐
A kiss on the cheek	☐	☐	☐	☐	☐
Flowers	☐	☐	☐	☐	☐
Movie tickets	☐	☐	☐	☐	☐
A gift certificate	☐	☐	☐	☐	☐
Clothing	☐	☐	☐	☐	☐
A meal at a restaurant	☐	☐	☐	☐	☐

Choices	Reasons
I would give chocolate to everybody...	because everybody likes it.
I wouldn't give money to anybody...	because it's too impersonal.
I would give a kiss to my mother, but not my boss...	because it's too personal.
I wouldn't give my mother a gift certificate, but I'd give one to my teacher...	because it's a good gift for someone you don't know well.

A.

B. *l*

C.

D.

E.

F.

► CUSTOMS FROM AROUND THE WORLD

A. Look at customs which are common in countries around the world. Match each custom with the correct picture.

1. People kissing on the cheek when they meet.
2. People expecting a tip for most services.
3. People bringing their dogs with them into restaurants.
4. People eating food from street stalls.
5. People eating food with their hands.
6. People sitting with legs crossed.

B. PAIR WORK. How do you feel about the customs above? Take turns asking about the customs and reacting to them. Use the model below.

A: How do you feel about **people kissing on the cheek...?**

B: *Its fine with me.*

A: Oh really?

   Well, how do you feel about...?

Expressing Opinions

It's fine with me.
I find it a bit strange.
I don't mind at all.
I don't like it at all.

Listen to people describing customs they observed while traveling overseas. Check (✔) the customs and reactions to the customs.

⭕ CUSTOMS

COUNTRY	CUSTOM		REACTION TO CUSTOM	
			Comfortable	Uncomfortable
1. 🇦🇺 Australia	✔ party	☐ dating	☐	☐
2. 🇫🇷 France	☐ gift giving	☐ greetings	☐	☐
3. 🇨🇳 China	☐ visiting	☐ meeting	☐	☐

► IMPORTANT CUSTOMS

GROUP WORK. What advice can you give a foreigner visiting your country about the customs listed? Discuss the customs and give advice. Use the model below.

CUSTOMS

1. Meeting someone for the first time.

2. Visiting someone's house.

3. Eating a meal with people at a restaurant.

4. Giving gifts.

5. Going to a wedding.

6. Going to a funeral.

	Giving Advice
A: What's a custom for **meeting someone for the first time?**	*You should always...* *You shouldn't...* *Sometimes it's a good idea to...*
B: *You should always* / *It's best to* / *It's polite to* shake hands.	*It's best to...* *It's common to...*
A: That's right. *And you shouldn't* / *It's impolite to* hug the person.	*It's* | *polite* / *impolite* | *to...*

AROUND TOWN

hang out with friends

watch videos

go surfing

sleep all day

surf the Internet

listen to music

► THE WEEKEND

A. PAIR WORK. Take turns asking your partner about these weekend activities. Choose follow-up questions from the list and use the model below.

A: Do you **hang out with friends** on the weekend?

B: Yeah, sometimes.

A: *Where do you* **hang out?**

B: Usually at coffee shops, especially Saturday nights and Sunday afternoons.

Follow-up Questions

Where do you…?

Who do you…with?

When do you…?

How | *often* / *long* | *do you…?*

B. GROUP WORK. Share your three favorite weekend activities. What is the most popular activity for your class?

One of my favorite activities is **sleeping all day.**
The activity I like best is **sleeping all day.**
Sleeping all day is what I like to do.

► **LISTENING** 🔲

Listen to different friends talking about weekend activities. Number the conversations as you listen.

► **ENTERTAINMENT CHOICES**

PAIR WORK. Take turns *asking about* and *reacting to* these activities. Add at least one of your own. Use the model below.

1. Going to a rock concert.
2. Going to a film festival.
3. Going to a comedy club.
4. Visiting the zoo.
5. Visiting an amusement park.

6. Seeing a magic show.
7. Seeing a tennis match.
8. Trying a new restaurant.
9. Trying bungee jumping.
10. _____

		Reactions
A: What do you think of / How about	**visiting the zoo?**	It sounds fantastic. It would be great. I'd love to.
B: *It sounds fantastic.* OR *It sounds boring.*		It sounds ⎰ OK. ⎱ boring.
A: Oh, good. Let's do it. OR Actually, I think it could be fun.		I'm not really interested in doing that.

hear live music at a nightclub

buy nice things at a reasonable price

eat tasty but inexpensive food

have a good cup of coffee

go to an outdoor concert

people watch

► HOT SPOTS

A. PAIR WORK. Where can you do the activities above? Take turns making suggestions and asking about other things you can do in your city.

	Suggestions
A: Where can you **hear live music?**	*A good place for that is...*
B: *A good place for that is* Rick's Cafe.	*I'd recommend...*
	I'd say...
A: Yes, that's true. *Another good place is* the Blue Note.	*Another good place is...*
	Or even better is...

B. GROUP WORK. Share your suggestions with the class. Which hot spots were suggested?

► LISTENING 🔲

Listen to Angela, Max, Ellen, and Charles talk about favorite hot spots in their city. Write their favorite *hot spot* and the *reason* it's their favorite in the chart.

	Hot Spot	Reason
1. Angela	*City Cafe*	*people watch*
2. Max		
3. Ellen		
4. Charles		

► THE BEST

A. GROUP WORK. Decide on the best places in town. Fill in the chart below.

THE BEST PLACES IN TOWN

Food	Shopping	Activities
Best place for ice cream	Best bookstore	Best amusement park
Best place for noodles	Best place to buy sports clothes	Best fitness center
Best place for pizza	Best gift shop	Best place to sing karaoke
Best place for lunch	Best discount store	Best movie theater
Best place for take-out food	Best department store	Best nightclub

B. Report your group's choices to the class.

We think **the best**	place for ice cream bookstore	is...

We didn't agree on Some people think Others feel that	the best...

MOVIES

A.

B. *1*

C.

D.

E.

F.

► MOVIE TALK

A. PAIR WORK. Can you identify the types of movies above? Match a movie type from the list below with a photo.

| 1. action | 2. romance | 3. drama | 4. sci-fi | 5. comedy | 6. animated |

| I think this one is a(n) | action
sci-fi
animated | movie. | Do you think it's a | romance?
drama?
comedy? |

B. GROUP WORK. Take turns asking and answering the movie survey questions.

1. What is your favorite type of movie?
2. Do you prefer seeing movies at a theater or at home?
3. How much do you spend a month on movies or videos?
4. Have you ever seen a movie more than twice? Which movie(s)?
5. Who are your two favorite movie stars?
6. Have you ever seen a movie star? Who?

A. PRE-LISTENING. Look at these questions about movies. What information does each question ask for? Match the questions with the correct information.

1. What kind of movie is it?
2. Who's in it?
3. What's it like?
4. Where's it playing?
5. Is it worth seeing?

☐ a recommendation
☐ description of the movie
☐ the actors and actresses
☑ the type of movie it is
☐ the theater where you can see it

B. Listen to a movie critic discussing movies. Check (✔) the correct information about each one.

☺ MOVIES

	TYPE OF MOVIE	GOOD POINTS	BAD POINTS	RATING
Movie 1	sci-fi ☐	acting ☐	soundtrack ☐	
	comedy ☐	story ☐	acting ☐	
	drama ☐	special effects ☐	story ☐	☐ ☐
Movie 2	comedy ☐	acting ☐	acting ☐	
	sci-fi ☐	story ☐	story ☐	
	romance ☐	special effects ☐	special effects ☐	☐ ☐
Movie 3	action ☐	acting ☐	acting ☐	
	horror ☐	story ☐	story ☐	
	drama ☐	soundtrack ☐	special effects ☐	☐ ☐

► MOVIE REVIEWS

GROUP WORK. Take turns describing a movie or video you've seen recently. Be sure to ask questions about the movies.

A: I saw *Silent Killer* the other day.
B: Oh, really? **What kind of movie is it?**
A: It's an *action movie*.
B: Oh. **Who's in it?**
A: Clint Eastwood.

B: Wow. **What's it like?**
A: It's *exciting* and it has *a good story*.

Describing Movies

exciting	sad	depressing
funny	moving	uplifting

	lots of action	good special effects
It has	a good story	a great soundtrack
	my favorite actor/actress in it	

A.

- They escape from the plane, but the pilot dies.

B. *1*

- Two people meet while on vacation in South America.

C.

- Their plane develops engine trouble.

D.

- They decide to take a sight-seeing trip in a small plane.

E.

- They realize they are a long way from civilization and have no food or drink.

F.

- The pilot crash lands the plane in the jungle.

▶ MOVIE SCENES

A. PAIR WORK. Look at these scenes from a movie. What do you think the story is about? Number the scenes in sequence from 1 to 6.

B. How does the movie end? Make up an ending for the movie and give the movie a title. Share your movie ending with the class.

	Story Sequence Expressions
First they make a big fire.	
Then they make smoke signals.	*First...*
After that another plane sees them.	*Then...*
Finally they escape from the jungle.	*After that* OR *Later...*
A good title for this movie is...	*Finally...*

► LISTENING 📼

Read the statements below. Then listen to Katherine describing the story of a movie she has seen. Circle *T* for true or *F* for false.

		TRUE	FALSE
1.	It's a sci-fi movie.	T	Ⓕ
2.	It's about a Russian scientist and a nuclear bomb.	T	F
3.	The story takes place in America.	T	F
4.	Some men are driving a train with the bomb on it.	T	F
5.	They will set the bomb off unless the police set free some prisoners.	T	F
6.	A TV reporter kills the gangsters before the bomb goes off.	T	F

► SCRIPT WRITERS

GROUP WORK. Look at the sketches for a movie. Arrange the sketches in any order and make up a story for the movie. Tell the story to the class.

A: This is a(n)...

B: The story takes place in...

C: I think...

A: First they... Then...

B: After that...

C: Finally...

Useful Questions

What type of movie is it?

Where does the story take place?

What do you think is happening here?

What happens first?

What happens after that?

How does the movie end?

PROJECT FILE

Each project in the **Springboard Project File** has you:

▶ **PLAN** an activity that you will do inside or outside of class.

▶ **DO** the activity and make something that you can show others.

▶ **SHARE** the finished product of your activity with other students.

Design a name card for exchanging personal information.

 TOOL BOX

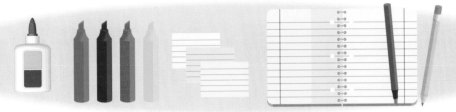

▶ PLAN

Write down information about yourself.

Name:	**Nickname:**
Date of Birth:	**Blood Type:**
Tel:	**Fax:**
Favorite Hobby:	
Food:	
Music:	

▶ DO

Design a name card choosing information from your chart above.

Name: *John Richardson*   Blood Type: *AB*

Address: *23 Mission Bay*   I like: *surfing*

Auckland, New Zealand   *Mexican food*

Tel: *(617) 639-0000*   *Rock music*

Fax: *same as phone*

▶ SHARE

A. Make copies for all of your classmates.

B. Exchange cards and place everyone's card in a notebook to make your own class Name Book.

PROJECT RAP SONG

Express yourselves through Rap, a popular music style that puts rhymes to music.

🔧 TOOL BOX

▶ PLAN

In a group decide on a topic that interests you. For example, dating or school.

▶ DO

A. Write down as many words and phrases related to the topic as you can in a list.

B. Below write rhyming words for words from your list. Words with the same ending sound rhyme. For example, *cool school, end friends, please overseas.*

_____ _____ , _____ _____

_____ _____ , _____ _____

C. Arrange the rhyming words and phrases and find a beat or rhythm.
D. Practice saying your rap to the beat.

▶ SHARE

Present your rap song to the class. If possible, record your rap song.

LEARNING ENGLISH

Learning English is really cool, that's why I come to school.

It's not my English teacher I'm trying to please. I just want to see my friends overseas.

PROJECT PERSONAL DICTIONARY

Build your own dictionary, a useful learning strategy for improving vocabulary and remembering words.

🔧 TOOL BOX

▶ **PLAN**

A. Write a list of new English words you hear in class in a small notebook.

B. Choose twenty words you would like to learn.

▶ **DO**

Make a dictionary study card for each word. Use the card samples below as a model.

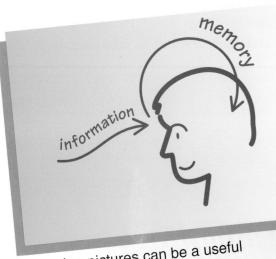

Drawing pictures can be a useful strategy for remembering words

Memorize/meməraiz—verb
To learn well enough to remember exactly

If you build your own vocabulary book, you can memorize many new words

Synonyms: remember, retain
Antonym: forget

Writing definitions and antonyms and synonyms is another useful strategy

▶ **SHARE**

A. Make copies of your cards for your classmates.

B. Present and explain your cards in small groups.

C. Select classmates' cards you would like to copy and add to your own dictionary.

PROJECT BEST UNIFORM

Find the best-looking work uniforms in your area.

🔧 TOOL BOX

▶ PLAN

Make a list of five places in your area where workers wear uniforms. For example, a hotel, department store, convenience store, or fast-food restaurant.

1. _____
2. _____
3. _____
4. _____
5. _____

▶ DO

A. Visit three of the places with a partner. Bring a notebook and, if possible, a camera.

B. Observe the staff at each place. Take notes and draw sketches, or take pictures.

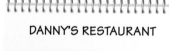

ROYAL HOTEL	DANNY'S RESTAURANT	LUCKY CONVENIENCE STORE
BELL HOPS	WAITERS	CASHIERS
navy pants	striped jacket	two-piece navy skirt and vest
white jacket	bow tie	white blouse
gold trim on jacket	navy pants	
red and gold cap		

C. Make a poster of the best-looking uniforms.

▶ SHARE

Report the results of your research to the class.

Plan and present the perfect dream trip.

🔧 TOOL BOX

▶ PLAN

A. Choose a place you would like to travel for your dream trip poster.

B. Make a list of at least three possible sources of information about the place you chose. For example, travel agencies, newspapers, and web sites.

1. _____   2. _____   3. _____

▶ DO

A. From the sources, find information about hotels, restaurants, sightseeing attractions, timetables, and cultural and sporting events for your dream trip.

B. Design a poster of your dream trip.

▶ SHARE

Present your poster and explain the trip to your class. Vote on the best dream trip.

PROJECT CELEBRITY DATING

Follow the lives of your favorite celebrities. Who do they date? Who are they married to? Design a poster to tell it all.

🔧 TOOL BOX

GOSSIP

▶ PLAN

Find pictures and information about your favorite celebrities in newspapers and entertainment magazines.

▶ DO

Make a celebrity poster.

Include:
- pictures of the celebrities
- biographical and career information
- information about their love lives
- any other interesting facts

▶ SHARE

Present your poster and explain the information to the class.

Brad Pitt

Born: 12/18/64 Shawnee, Oklahoma USA
Home: Los Angeles, CA
Former job: Dressed as a giant chicken for a restaurant
First Movie: Cutting Class
*Brad is dating Gwyneth Paltrow

Sandra Bullock

Born: 7/26/66 Washington, DC USA
Home: Brentwood, CA
Hobbies: Surfing the Internet
First Movie: A Fool and His Money
*Sandra is currently single

PROJECT INTERNATIONAL FOOD FAIR

Spaghetti comes from Italy, chocolate from Switzerland, kimchi from Korea. How many countries does the food you eat come from?

TOOL BOX

▶ PLAN

A. Make a list of some of the international foods you eat.

B. Photocopy the map on page 73 and mount it on a poster board.

▶ DO

A. Collect labels and wrappers from various bottles, boxes, jars, and cans your international food comes in.

B. Prepare an information card about each food item. Use the model below.

Country ▶	Switzerland
Type of food ▶	Chocolate
Price ▶	$2.50
Where it was bought ▶	International Market

▶ SHARE

A. Group the labels by country and attach them with the information card to the map's border. Draw a line to connect the labels and cards with the country.

B. Present your map in small groups.

NEW ZEALAND

Kiwi fruit
5 for $2.00
Fruit stand

BRAZIL

Coffee
$7.00 a bag
World Market

WHOLE
BEAN
COFFEE

ITALY

Olive oil
$15.00
Bertucci's

PROJECT MYSTERY PERSON

Make a collage to introduce yourself visually.

🔧 TOOL BOX

▶ PLAN

Write down information about yourself.

FAVORITES		FACTS
Movie _____	Clothing _____	Personality Type _____
Book _____	Music _____	Blood Type _____
Hobby _____	Celebrity _____	Horoscope Sign _____

▶ DO

A. Collect photos from magazines and items that show your personality.

B. Make a collage, but don't put your name on it.

▶ SHARE

A. Display all collages in class with blank sheets of paper next to them.

B. Write comments and guess the makers of the collages.

PROJECT BUSINESS VENTURE

Put your skills to good use by starting a new business.

 TOOL BOX

▶ PLAN

A. Make a list of three skills that you have. Look at the examples in the chart below.

Skills *example:* good at computers

1. _____ 2. _____ 3. _____

▶ DO

A. In small groups decide how you can use the members' skills to start a new business.

B. Decide on a job and job title for each member. Use the model below.

	MIKE	JOHN	JANE	SUE
SKILLS	good at computers	great cook	excellent driver	math whiz
JOB	design web page	make pizza	deliver pizza	control money
JOB TITLE	Computer Specialist	Cook	Driver	Accountant

C. Design a publicity poster to promote your business.

▶ SHARE

Present your poster and explain your business venture to the class.

PROJECT AROUND THE WORLD AT HOME

Look around your town at different products and customs. How much influence do other cultures have on your own?

🔧 TOOL BOX

▶ PLAN

Make a chart like the one below and write as many examples of products and customs from other countries as you can. Then write where you are most likely to see them.

	Item	Other country	Where in town?
Clothes			
Customs			
Food			

▶ DO

A. Walk around your town with a partner and take photos or draw sketches of the items you included in the chart.

B. Write notes for each photo or sketch. Use the model below.

• Influence of fast food from the United States
• McDonald's in downtown Beijing

▶ SHARE

Display the photos or sketches with the captions on a poster board. Look at your classmates' posters and list your three favorite products and customs from other countries. Are they similar to or different from your classmates?

Plan a fun weekend around town for a foreign visitor staying at your home.

TOOL BOX

► **PLAN**

Make a list of fun, interesting activities and "hot spots" for visitors to your town.

Cultural Activities	Shopping	Restaurants	Events and Fitness Activities
Bolshoi Ballet	Bargain House	Top of the City	swim and sauna

► **DO**

Plan a two-day schedule. Decide the following:
- where you will go and why
- how you will get there
- how long you will spend at each place
- how much it will all cost

► **SHARE**

Make copies of your schedule and explain your weekend in small groups.

DAY 1   **DAY 2**

9:00 Plaza for brunch. Walk. About an hour. Cost: $25.⁰⁰

10:00 Hockney Exhibition. Subway. About 2 hours. Cost: $8.⁰⁰

12:00

PROJECT FREEZE FRAME

Write a screenplay with classmates and enter it in a class screenplay festival.

🔧 TOOL BOX

▶ PLAN

In small groups choose one of the photos below to use in your screenplay.

▶ DO

A. Write a screenplay for a two to four minute movie. In the opening or closing scene, you must recreate the pose in the photo you have chosen.

B. Rehearse your screenplay with your group members.

C. Videotape your screenplay if you have a video camera.

▶ SHARE

A. Present your videotape or perform your play.

B. Ask your classmates to fill out a Movie Screenplay Survey like the one below to determine the winner of the class screenplay festival.

🎬 SCREENPLAY CRITIC NOTES

	RATING
Movie name:	
Type of movie:	
Actors/Actresses:	
Good Points:	
Bad Points	

GLOSSARY

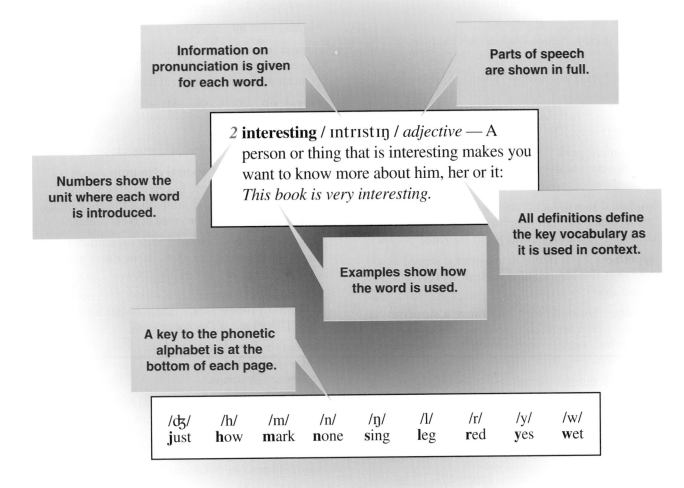

Information on pronunciation is given for each word.

Parts of speech are shown in full.

2 **interesting** / ɪntrɪstɪŋ / *adjective* — A person or thing that is interesting makes you want to know more about him, her or it: *This book is very interesting.*

Numbers show the unit where each word is introduced.

All definitions define the key vocabulary as it is used in context.

Examples show how the word is used.

A key to the phonetic alphabet is at the bottom of each page.

/ʤ/	/h/	/m/	/n/	/ŋ/	/l/	/r/	/y/	/w/
just	how	mark	none	sing	leg	red	yes	wet

The ***Springboard* Glossary** defines key vocabulary from the units and gives examples of how the words are used.

Use the ***Springboard* Glossary** to:

▶ Learn the meanings of key vocabulary words from the book.

▶ See examples of how key vocabulary words are used in context.

▶ Learn how key vocabulary words are pronounced.

4 **accessory** / ɪksesəri / *noun* — **fashion accessory** — jewelry, scarves and handbags are fashion accessories.

1 **action movie** / ækʃən muvi / *noun* — a movie with a lot of excitement: *I like action movies because they are never boring.*

12 **actor** / æktər / *noun* — a man who acts in a movie.

12 **actress** / æktrəs / *noun* — a woman who acts in a movie.

4 **all right** / ɔl rait / *adverb, adjective* — not bad, ordinary.

6 **amusement park** / əmyuzment pɑrk / *noun* — an open area with rides, shows, etc.: *Disneyland is an amusement park.*

12 **animated movie** / ænəmeitɪd muvi / *noun* — a movie made by photographing a series of drawings: *Disney is famous for its animated movies.*

7 **appetizer** / æpətaizər / *noun* — food served as a course at the beginning of a meal: *Olives make a simple appetizer.*

10 **arrange** / əreindʒ / *verb* — **arrange a surprise party** — plan an unexpected party for someone: *The secretary at our office arranged a surprise party for the manager's birthday.*

1 **athletic** / æθletɪk / *adjective* — physically strong, healthy and active: *She looks very athletic.*

4 **attractive** / ətræktɪv / *adjective* — nice to look at: *Her shoes are attractive.*

4 **average** / ævrɪdʒ / *adjective* — ordinary or usual.

4 **awesome** / ɔsəm / *adjective (informal U.S.)* — excellent; great: *Did you see Sue's outfit — she looks awesome.*

2 **beautiful** / byutəfəl / *adjective* — very nice; pleasing to see or hear.

9 **benefits** / benəfɪts / *noun (plural)* — **job benefits** — extras, given to a company employee in addition to salary or wages: *Company health insurance is a job benefit.*

1 **blood type** / bləd taip / *noun* — the red liquid inside your body which comes in types "O", "A", "B", and "AB".

2 **boring** / bɔrɪŋ / *adjective* — not interesting: *That lesson was boring!*

9 **boss** / bɔs / *noun* — a person who controls a place where people work and tells people what they must do: *I asked my boss for a day off.*

6 **brainy** / breini / *adjective* — very smart; intelligent.

4 **brand name** / brænd neim / *noun* — the company name of a thing you buy: *'Harley Davidson' is a famous brand name for motorcycles.*

6 **break up** / breik əp / *verb* — (~ with somebody) — stop being with somebody, for example a husband or wife, boyfriend or girlfriend: *Kathy broke up with her boyfriend last week.*

11 **bungee jumping** / bəndʒi dʒəmpiŋ / *noun* — sport in which people fasten an elastic rope around their legs and jump off a tower or bridge: *Bungee jumping was invented in New Zealand.*

7 **calorie (count)** / kæləri / *noun* — a unit of energy supplied by food: *A calorie count shows the number of calories in a serving of food.*

4 **casual** / kæʒuəl / *adjective* — not for serious or important times: *I wear casual clothes such as jeans and T-shirts when I'm not at work.*

10 **celebrate** / seləbreit / *verb* — to enjoy oneself on a special day or event: *On December 25 we celebrate Christmas.*

7 **cereals** / sɪriəlz / *noun (plural)* — plants that farmers grow so that we can eat the seed: *Wheat and oats are cereals.*

9 **challenging** / tʃæləndʒɪŋ / *adjective* — difficult; demanding: *Being a doctor is challenging.*

10 **cheek** / tʃik / *noun* — one of the two round parts of your face under your eyes: *When friends meet, they kiss each other on the cheek.*

12 **civilization** / sɪvəlɪzeiʃən / *noun* — the comfortable conditions of modern life: *be a long way from civilization* (= far from a town or city).

2 **classical music** / klæsɪkəl myuzik / *noun* — music in a traditional style usually performed by an orchestra: *Mozart is a famous composer of classical music.*

4 **classy** / klæsi / *adjective* — high quality, expensive and stylish.

/i/	/ɪ/	/e/	/æ/	/ɑ/	/ɔ/	/ʊ/	/u/	/ə/	/ei/
see	sit	bet	hat	hot	talk	book	too	above	face

8 **clever** / klevər/ *adjective* — able to learn, understand or do something quickly and well: *a clever student.*

12 **comedy** / kɑmədi / *noun* — a funny movie or play.

11 **comedy club** / kɑmədi kləb / *noun* — a nightclub where the customers are entertained by people telling jokes and funny stories.

4 **comfort** / kəmfərt / *noun* — a feeling of ease and relaxation: *Comfort is important when choosing clothes.*

4 **comfortable** / kəmftərbəl / *adjective* — nice to wear or be in: *This is a very comfortable shirt.*

10 **comfortable (with)** / kəmftərbəl / *verb* — to feel free from difficulty or worry: *I am very comfortable with the American style of business* ☆ opposite: **uncomfortable (with)**.

3 **comic book** / kɑmɪk bʊk/ *noun* — a magazine with pictures that tell a story.

3 **common expression** / kɑmən ɪkspreʃən / *noun* — a phrase that is often said or heard: *'How are you?' is a common English expression.*

9 **communicator** / kəmyunɪkeitər / *noun* — **good communicator** — someone with the ability to express ideas clearly: *He is a good communicator.*

9 **company reputation** / kəmpəni repyəteiʃən / *noun* — what people think or say about a company: *Sony has a good company reputation.*

7 **convenience store** / kənvinyəns stɔr / *noun* — a shop that sells food and various other items and stays open longer than other shops.

4 **cool** / kul / *adjective* (*informal*) — good; interesting; excellent; stylish: *Torn jeans are cool.* • *Have you met Tom yet — he's really cool.*

2 **country music** / kəntri myuzɪk / *noun* — music in the folk style of the southern or western US.

3 **course** / kɔrs / *noun* — a series of lessons: *My university courses each last 20 weeks.*

8 **creative** / krieitɪv / *adjective* — having a lot of new ideas or being good at making new things: *She's a very good painter — she's so creative.*

8 **critical** / krɪtɪkəl / *adjective* — If you are critical of somebody or something, you say that they are wrong or bad: *They were very critical of my work.*

8 **criticize** / krɪtəsaiz / *verb* — to tell someone about their faults: *My boss always criticizes me about my work habits.*

6 **culture** / kəltʃər / *noun* — the way of life of a group of people: *She is studying Chinese culture.*

6 **cute** / kyut / *adjective* — attractive; pretty and charming.

7 **daily** / deili / *adjective, adverb* — done or happening everyday: *People should eat fruit daily.*

8 **daydream** / deidrim / *verb* — to have pleasant thoughts about something you would rather be doing: *She always daydreams in class.*

8 **decisive** / dɪsaisɪv / *adjective* — having the ability or power to decide: *My boss is a decisive person.*

12 **depressing** / dɪpresɪŋ / *adjective* — Something that is depressing makes you very unhappy: *That movie about the war was very depressing.*

1 **designer clothes** / dɪzainər klouz / *noun* (plural) — shirts, pants, dresses, etc. that are made by a famous designer: *Designer clothes are usually expensive.*

3 **develop** / dɪveləp / *verb* — improve or make better: *A salesman must develop good communication skills.*

7 **diet** / daiɪt / *noun* — the food you eat: *It is important to have a healthy diet.*

3 **difficult** / dɪfəkəlt / *adjective* — not easy to do or understand: *a difficult job.*

11 **discount store** / dɪskaunt stɔr / *noun* — a shop that sells different types of goods at low prices: *Shopping at a discount store can save a lot of money.*

12 **drama** / drɑmə / *noun* — a movie with an emotional story.

1 **driver's license** / draivərz laisəns / *noun* — a piece of paper that shows you are allowed to drive a car.

6 **(go) Dutch** / dətʃ / *verb* — share expenses: *Let's go Dutch and each pay for our own meal.*

9 **easy** / izi / *adjective* — simple; not difficult.

1 **easygoing** / izigoɪŋ / *adjective* — (of persons) pleasant; casual: *He is an easygoing person.*

3 **e-mail** / i meiəl / *noun* — "e"lectronic mail sent over the Internet.

/ou/	/ai/	/au/	/ɔi/	/p/	/b/	/t/	/d/	/k/	/g/
home	five	out	boy	pen	bad	ten	dog	cat	got

8 **emotional** / ɪmouʃənəl / *adjective* — If you are emotional, you have strong feelings and you show them: *He got very emotional when we said good-bye.*

8 **energetic** / enərdʒetɪk / *adjective* — full of energy so that you can do a lot of things.

12 **escape** / ɪskeip / *verb* — (~ from) get free from somewhere, somebody or something: *The bird escaped from the cage.*

9 **exciting** / ɪksaitɪŋ / *adjective* — Something that is exciting makes you have strong feelings of happiness or interest: *an exciting movie.*

9 **exhausting** / ɪgzɔstɪŋ / *adjective* — making one feel very tired: *Delivering pizzas on a busy night is exhausting.*

9 **factor** / fæktər / *noun* — any of the things that cause or influence something: *Salary and working hours are important factors to think about when choosing a job.*

11 **fantastic** / fæntæstɪk / *adjective* — very good; wonderful: *We had a fantastic vacation.*

1 **favorite** / feivərɪt / *adjective* — most liked: *Red is my favorite color.*

11 **film festival** / fɪlm festɪvəl / *noun* — a series of movies shown as a special event, usually once a year: *Cannes, France has the world's most famous film festival.*

11 **fitness center** / fɪtnɪs sentər / *noun* — a building with exercise machines and workout areas for members: *I work out at the fitness center every other day.*

4 **flannel** / flænəl / *noun* — soft woolen or cotton cloth: *a flannel shirt.*

7 **flavor** / fleivər / *noun* — the unique taste that each food has: *Coffee is my favorite flavor of ice cream.*

8 **flexible** / fleksəbəl / *adjective* — changing easily: *It's not important to me when we go — my plans are quite flexible.*

4 **formal** / fɔrməl / *adjective* — important or serious times that require special dress and manners: *I wore a suit and tie because it was a formal dinner.*

8 **frustrated** / frəstreitɪd / *adjective* — If you are frustrated, something makes you angry because you cannot do what you want to do: *I get frustrated when I can't say what I mean in a foreign language.*

5 **fun** / fən / *adjective* — something pleasureable; enjoyable: *Skiing is fun.*

10 **funeral** / fyunərəl / *noun* — a ceremony for a person who has recently died: *I went to my neighbor's funeral.*

12 **funny** / fəni / *adjective* — A person or a thing that is funny makes you laugh or smile: *a funny story.*

1 **gamble** / gæmbəl / *verb* — try to win money by playing games that need luck: *He gambled a lot of money at the horse track.*

12 **gangster** / gæŋstər / *noun* — one of a group of dangerous criminals: *Al Capone was a famous Chicago gangster.*

8 **generous** / dʒenərəs / *adjective* — always ready to give things or to spend money: *She is very generous — she often buys me presents.*

3 **get along with** / get əlɔŋ wɪθ / *verb* — (~ with somebody) to have a comfortable or friendly relationship with somebody: *I really like my class because I get along with everybody.*

10 **gift certificate** / gɪft sərtɪfəkɪt / *noun* — a piece of paper, usually given as a present, which can be exchanged in a shop for goods: *For Christmas, I received a $50.00 gift certificate to use at my favorite store.*

6 **going steady** / gouɪŋ stedi / *verb* — (~ with somebody) to be dating somebody seriously: *I have been going steady with Jane for 6 months.*

6 **gorgeous** / gɔrdʒəs / *adjective* — beautiful; wonderful; good-looking: *What a gorgeous dress!*

11 **hang out** / hæŋ aut / *verb* — stay somewhere with nothing special to do: *My friends and I like to hang out at the video arcade.*

9 **hard** / hɑrd / *adjective* — difficult; not easy.

8 **hard-working** / hɑrd wərkɪŋ / *adjective* — to be very serious about your work and work long hours: *The people in my office are all hard-working.*

6 **homebody** / houmbɑdi / *noun* — a person who is comfortable at home and doesn't like to go out very much.

5 **honeymoon** / hənimun / *noun* — a vacation that a man and woman have just after they get married: *My parents went to Hawaii on their honeymoon.*

/f/	/v/	/θ/	/ð/	/s/	/z/	/ʃ/	/ʒ/	/tʃ/
fall	**v**an	**th**in	**th**en	**s**un	**z**oo	**sh**e	vi**s**ion	**ch**in

2 **horrible** / hɔrəbəl / *adjective* — very bad: *a horrible movie.*

11 **hot spot** / hɑt spɑt / *noun* — an exciting, popular place to go: *The new disco is my favorite hot spot.*

5 **ideal** / aidiəl / *adjective* — the best or exactly right: *This is an ideal place for a picnic.*

8 **impatient** / ɪmpeiʃənt / *adjective* — not patient: (see "patient").

10 **impersonal** / ɪmpərsənəl / *adjective* — not personal: (see "personal").

10 **impolite** / ɪmpəlait / *adjective* — not polite: (see "polite").

11 **inexpensive** / ɪnəkspensiv / *adjective* — cheap; not expensive: *Something that doesn't cost a lot of money is inexpensive.*

2 **interesting** / ɪntrɪstɪŋ / *adjective* — A person or thing that is interesting makes you want to know more about him, her or it: *This book is very interesting.*

3 **Internet** / ɪntərnet / *noun* — an electronic exchange of information and mail by a large computer network: *Our class uses the Internet to research information for projects.*

2 **jazz music** / dʒæz myuzik / *noun* — music of African-American origin with strong rhythms that are freely developed during a performance: *New Orleans is famous for jazz music.*

9 **job satisfaction** / dʒɑb sætisfækʃən / *noun* — to be happy doing your job: *Job satisfaction is an important factor when choosing a job.*

9 **job security** / dʒɑb sɪkyʊrəti / *noun* — the feeling that you can work at your current company for as long as you want: *Working for the government gives you job security.*

12 **jungle** / dʒəŋgəl / *noun* — a thick forest in a hot part of the world: *There are jungles in South America.*

2 **karaoke** / kæriouki / *noun* — recorded music of a popular song without the singer's voice: *People use karaoke to sing along with a song.*

8 **keep (one's) word** / kip wənz werd / *verb* — to do what you say you are going to do: *Tom is reliable, he always keeps his word.*

8 **lazy** / leizi / *adjective* — not wanting to work: *Don't be so lazy — come and help me!*

3 **life-long** / laif lɔŋ / *adjective* — continuing or lasting for a lifetime.

2 **lively** / laivli / *adjective* — cheerful and full of interest or excitement: *Brazilian music is very lively.*

5 **lobster** / lɑbstər / *noun* — a large shellfish with eight legs and two large claws: *Lobsters turn bright red when you cook them.*

2 **lonely** / lounli / *adjective* — alone and without friends: *I've been lonely since my family moved to a new city.*

4 **look** / lʊk / *noun* — the way something seems: *Wearing torn jeans and a white T-shirt with a leather jacket is a great look.*

6 **looks** / lʊks / *noun* (no plural) — a person's appearance or features: *Models have good looks.*

2 **loud** / laud / *adjective* — noisy; easily heard: *Rock music is often very loud.*

11 **magic show** / mædʒik ʃou / *noun* — a performance of mysterious tricks: *At the magic show I saw a man escape from a cage.*

9 **manage** / mænidʒ / *verb* — control somebody or something: *She manages a department of 30 people.*

6 **manners** / mænərz / *noun* (plural) — the way you behave when you are with other people: *It's bad manners to talk with your mouth full.*

7 **Mediterranean** / medətəreiniən / *noun* — the Mediterranean Sea and the countries around it.

10 **memorable** / memərəbəl / *adjective* — easy to remember because it is special in some way: *Their wedding was a very memorable day.*

12 **moving** / muviŋ / *adjective* — causing strong feelings: *The movie is a moving story about a young boy's fight against AIDS.*

6 **nature** / neitʃər / *noun* — (no plural) everything in the world that was not made by people: *the beauty of nature.*

4 **neat** / nit / *adjective* (informal) — **kind of neat** — good; all right: *That idea is kind of neat.*

2 **New Age music** / nu eidʒ myuzik / *noun* — a relaxing style of music that combines the instruments and rhythms of many different cultures.

/dʒ/	/h/	/m/	/n/	/ŋ/	/l/	/r/	/y/	/w/
just	**h**ow	**m**ark	**n**one	si**ng**	**l**eg	**r**ed	**y**es	**w**et

2 **nice** / naɪs / *adjective* — pleasant, fine: *a nice day.*

1 **nickname** / nɪkneɪm / *noun* — an informal name used by friends and family instead of someone's real or full name.

5 **night spots** / naɪt spɑts / *noun* (plural) — places to go at night for eating, drinking and entertainment.

2 **nothing special** / nəθɪŋ speʃəl / *noun* — ordinary; usual: *That movie was nothing special.*

12 **nuclear bomb** / nukliər bɑm / *noun* — a weapon that uses the great power that is made by breaking or joining parts of atoms.

4 **old-fashioned** / ould fæʃənd / *adjective* — not modern; not worn often: *Clothes from the 1920's look old-fashioned now.*

4 **outdated** / autdeitɪd / *adjective* — not useful or common any more; old-fashioned: *A lot of computer equipment is getting outdated.*

3 **overseas** / ouvərsiz / *adjective, adverb* — in, to or from another country across the sea: *There are many students from Korea studying overseas.*

1 **party animal** / pɑrti æniməl / *noun* — a person who loves parties and goes to them as often as possible: *Bill loves to have fun — he is a real party animal.*

3 **pass** / pæs / *verb* — **pass an exam** — do well enough on an examination or test; not fail: *Did you pass your driving exam?*

7 **pasta** / pɑstə / *noun* — Italian noodles which come in many shapes and types: *Spaghetti and lasagna are kinds of pasta.*

8 **patient** / peiʃənt / *adjective* — to be calm and not get angry even in a difficult situation: *It is important for parents to be patient with their children.* ☆ opposite: **impatient**.

1 **pepperoni pizza** / pepərouni pitsə / *noun* — a pizza with spicy sausage used as a topping.

10 **personal** / pərsənəl / *adjective* — done or made for a particular person: *This letter is personal, so I don't want anyone else to read it.* ☆ opposite: **impersonal**.

8 **personality trait** / pərsənæləti treit / *noun* — part of somebody's character; a personal quality: *Patience and creativity are personality traits.*

9 **persuasive** / pərsweisɪv / *adjective* — able to make somebody do or believe something: *The salesperson was very persuasive.*

3 **point of view** / pɔintəvyu / *noun* — the way a person thinks about something: *I understand your point of view.*

10 **polite** / pəlait / *adjective* — helpful and kind to other people: *It is polite to say 'please' when you ask for something.* ☆ opposite: **impolite**.

6 **politics** / pɑlətiks / *noun* — business or matters concerned with government: *Reading about politics is my hobby.*

7 **poultry** / poultri / *noun* — birds kept for their eggs and meat: *Chickens, ducks and geese are poultry.*

4 **pretty good** / prɪti gʊd / *adjective* — not bad; all right.

4 **price** / prais / *noun* — how much money you pay to buy something: *The price is $15.*

12 **prisoner** / prizənər / *noun* — a person who is in prison (a place where criminals are kept).

4 **quality** / kwɑləti / *noun* (no plural) — how good or bad something is: *This watch isn't very good quality.*

2 **rap music** / ræp myuzik / *noun* — a kind of music in which singers speak the words of a song very quickly.

11 **reasonable** / rizənəbəl / *adjective* — fair and right: *I think $20 dollars is a reasonable price.*

11 **recommend** / rekəmend / *verb* — tell somebody that another person or thing is good or useful: *Can you recommend a good hotel near the airport?*

1 **reggae music** / regeɪ myuzik / *noun* — a type of West Indian music: *Bob Marley was a famous reggae singer.*

2 **relaxing** / rɪlæksɪŋ / *adjective* — something that helps you to be rested and calm: *New age music is very relaxing.*

8 **reliable** / rɪlaiəbəl / *adjective* — somebody or something that you can trust: *My car is very reliable.* ☆ opposite: **unreliable**.

1 **remember** / rɪmembər / *verb* — not to forget something: *Can you remember his name?*

/i/	/ɪ/	/e/	/æ/	/ɑ/	/ɔ/	/ʊ/	/u/	/ə/	/ei/
see	**sit**	**bet**	**hat**	**hot**	**talk**	**book**	**too**	**above**	**face**

3 **required** / rɪkwaiərd / *adjective* — If something is required, you must do it; necessary: *Is English a required course?*

9 **resort** / rɪzɔrt / *noun* — a place where a lot of people go on vacation: *a famous ski resort.*

2 **rock music** / rɑk myuzɪk / *noun* — a kind of modern music with a strong beat, usually played on electric guitars: *My father hates rock music.*

12 **romance** / roumæns / *noun* — a movie with a love story: *When I am lonely I like to watch a good romance.*

9 **salary** / sæləri / *noun* — money you receive regularly for work that you do.

4 **sandals** / sændəlz / *noun* (plural) — light open shoes that you wear in warm weather: *a pair of sandals.*

12 **sci-fi movie** / sai fai muvi / (**science fiction**) *noun* — a movie about things such as travel in space, life on other planets or life in the future: *Star Wars is a famous sci-fi movie.*

9 **self-employed** / self ɪmplɔɪd / *adjective* — working for yourself; having your own business.

6 **sense of humor** / sens əv hyumər / *noun* — the ability to laugh and make other people laugh at funny things: *Dave has a good sense of humor.*

8 **serious** / sɪriəs / *adjective* — thoughtful; not silly: *He is a serious person — he doesn't joke around.*

6 **sexy** / seksi / *adjective* — attractive in a sexual way: *Bikinis are sexy swimwear.*

3 **skill** / skɪl / *noun* — a thing that you can do well: *What skills do you need for this job?*

4 **sloppy** / slɑpi / *adjective* — careless or messy: *a sloppy dresser.*

12 **smoke signal** / smouk sɪgnəl / *noun* — a cloud, made by something burning, used to send a message.

7 **snack** / snæk / *noun* — a small amount of food, usually eaten between meals: *We had a snack on the train.*

5 **snorkeling** / snɔrkəlɪŋ / *noun* — the sport of swimming with a snorkel (a long tube swimmers use to breathe underwater).

6 **social life** / souʃəl laif / *noun* — time you spend with people after school or work: *Anne has a busy social life.*

4 **so-so** / sou sou / *adjective* — ordinary; OK.

2 **soundtrack** / saundtræk / *noun* — the recorded sound and music from a movie.

12 **special effects** / speʃəl ɪfekts / *noun* (plural) — things or noises (usually in a movie) that look or sound real, but that are actually man made: *The movie 'Jurassic Park' has great special effects.*

10 **special event** / speʃəl ɪvent / *noun* — a planned social occasion that is important: *The Olympics is a special event.*

2 **strange** / streindʒ / *adjective* — unusual or surprising: *Bagpipes have a strange sound if you have never heard them before.*

3 **strategy** / strætɪdʒi / *noun* — a plan that you use in order to do something: *a strategy to learn English.*

10 **street stall** / strit stɔl / *noun* — a table or small shop with an open front from which things are sold in a market, in a railway station, etc.: *Last night we ate dinner at a street stall.*

8 **stressed out** / strest aut / *adjective* — a feeling of worry because of problems in your life: *She's stressed out because she's got too much work to do.*

9 **stressful** / stresfəl / *adjective* — causing worry or nervous feelings: *She got sick because her job is very stressful.*

4 **stylish** / stailɪʃ / *adjective* — in fashion; in a fashionable style: *Her clothes are always stylish.*

9 **subscription** / səbskrɪpʃən / *noun* — money that you pay to get a newspaper or magazine delivered to your home.

11 **(go) surfing** / sərfɪŋ / *verb* — riding on waves using a surfboard: *I go surfing with my friends on weekends.*

11 **surf the Internet** / sərf ðə ɪntərnet / *verb* — using a computer to explore the Internet: *My hobby is surfing the Internet.*

4 **suspenders** / səspendərz / *noun* (plural) — a pair of straps, worn over your shoulders, for holding up your pants: *He uses suspenders instead of a belt.*

/ou/	/ai/	/au/	/ɔi/	/p/	/b/	/t/	/d/	/k/	/g/
home	**fi**ve	**ou**t	**boy**	**p**en	**b**ad	**t**en	**d**og	**c**at	**g**ot

4 **tacky** / tæki / *adjective* (*informal*) — cheap and of poor quality: *tacky clothes.*

11 **take-out food** / teik aut fud / *noun* — cooked food sold to be taken away and eaten somewhere else.

11 **tasty** / teisti / *adjective* — good to eat: *The soup was very tasty.*

2 **techno music** / teknou myuzik / *noun* — a type of music, popular at discos and night clubs, that has a heavy bass beat and is good for dancing.

8 **temper** / tempər / *noun* — **lose one's temper** — If you lose your temper, you get angry and cannot control what you say: *I was so angry, I lost my temper.*

2 **terrible** / terəbəl / *adjective* — very bad: *She had a terrible accident.* • *The food in that restaurant is terrible.*

6 **terrific** / tərıfık / *adjective* — very good; wonderful: *What a terrific idea!*

10 **tip** / tıp / *noun* — a small, extra amount of money given to somebody in exchange for a service, for example a waiter or taxi-driver: *I left a tip on the table.*

9 **tiring** / taiərıŋ / *adjective* — If something is tiring, it makes you tired: *a tiring job.*

4 **torn jeans** / tɔrn dʒinz / *noun* — jeans with a sloppy hole or holes in them: *Torn jeans are cool.*

1 **travel abroad** / trævəl əbrɔd / *verb* — to go to a country overseas: *I traveled abroad during my last summer vacation.*

9 **travel opportunities** / trævəl apərtunətiz / *noun* (plural) — having chances to go on trips: *I like my new job because I have many travel opportunities.*

5 **trolley** / trali / *noun* (US) — a bus powered by electricity from a cable above the street: *A trolley is the same as a streetcar or tram.*

4 **ugly** / əgli / *adjective* — not pretty to look at: *an ugly dog.*

6 **unacceptable** / ənıkseptəbəl / *adjective* — not good enough; not acceptable: *It's unacceptable to make so many mistakes.*

10 **uncomfortable (with)** / ənkəmftərbəl / *verb* — not comfortable with: (see "comfortable (with)").

8 **unrealistic** / ənriəlıstık / *adjective* — not accepting the facts of a situation; not realistic.

8 **unreliable** / ənrılaiəbəl / *adjective* — not reliable: (see "reliable").

5 **unusual** / ənyuʒuəl / *adjective* — something that does not happen often; not usual: *An African safari is an unusual vacation.*

12 **uplifting** / əplıftıŋ / *adjective* — giving the feeling of hope and happiness: *The end of the movie was uplifting.*

3 **useful** / yusfəl / *adjective* — good and helpful for doing something: *Math is a useful subject to learn.*

8 **vain** / vein / *adjective* — too proud of what you can do or how you look: *He is always looking at himself in the mirror — he is very vain.*

6 **video arcade** / vıdiou arkeid / *noun* — a building or shop that has a collection of video games; a game center: *Many teenagers like to hang out at video arcades.*

2 **vocalist** / voukəlıst / *noun* — a singer, especially in a rock or jazz group.

9 **volunteer** / valəntır / *noun* — a person who offers to do a job, usually without pay: *He is a volunteer at the hospital.*

8 **waste** / weist / *verb* — **waste time** — use too much time to do or make something: *Don't waste my time with stupid questions.*

4 **waterproof** / wɔtərpruf / *verb* — If something is waterproof, it doesn't let water go through it: *a waterproof jacket.*

8 **well-organized** / wel ɔrgənaizd / *adjective* — efficient; arranged and controlled: *a well-organized person.*

5 **wild** / waiəld / *adjective* — Wild plants and animals live or grow in nature, not with people: *wild flowers.*

8 **wise** / waiz / *adjective* — A person who is wise knows and understands a lot about many things: *a wise, old man.*

12 **worth** / wərθ / *adverb* — **worth seeing** — good or useful enough to do or have: *Is this movie worth seeing?*

/f/	/v/	/θ/	/ð/	/s/	/z/	/ʃ/	/ʒ/	/tʃ/
fall	**v**an	**th**in	**th**en	**s**un	**z**oo	**sh**e	vi**s**ion	**ch**in

Unit 1 Getting Started
action movie
athletic
blood type
designer clothes
driver's license
easygoing
favorite
gamble
nickname
party animal
pepperoni pizza
reggae music
remember
travel abroad

Unit 2 Music
beautiful
boring
classical music
country music
horrible
interesting
jazz music
karaoke
lively
lonely
loud
New Age music
nice
nothing special
rap music
relaxing
rock music
soundtrack
strange
techno music
terrible
vocalist

Unit 3 Learning for Life
comic book
common expression
course
develop
difficult
e-mail
get along with
Internet
life-long
overseas
pass (pass an exam)
point of view
required
skill
strategy
useful

Unit 4 Fashion
accessory (fashion accessory)
all right
attractive
average
awesome
brand name
casual
classy
comfort
comfortable
cool
flannel
formal
look
neat (kind of neat)
old-fashioned
outdated
pretty good
price
quality
sandals

sloppy
so-so
stylish
suspenders
tacky
torn jeans
ugly
waterproof

Unit 5 Great Escapes
fun
honeymoon
ideal
lobster
night spots
snorkeling
trolley
unusual
wild

Unit 6 Dating
amusement park
brainy
break up
culture
cute
(go) Dutch
going steady
gorgeous
homebody
looks
manners
nature
politics
sense of humor
sexy
social life
terrific
unacceptable
video arcade

Unit 7 Food for Thought
appetizer
calorie (count)
cereals
convenience store
daily
diet
flavor
Mediterranean
pasta
poultry
snack

Unit 8 Personalities
clever
creative
critical
criticize
daydream
decisive
emotional
energetic
flexible
frustrated
generous
hard-working
impatient
keep (one's) word
lazy
patient
personality trait
reliable
serious
stressed out
temper (lose one's temper)
unrealistic
unreliable
vain
waste (waste time)
well-organized
wise

Unit 9 Career Dreams
benefits (job benefits)
boss
challenging
communicator (good communicator)
company reputation
easy
exciting
exhausting
factor
hard
job satisfaction
job security
manage
persuasive
resort
salary
self-employed
stressful
subscription
tiring
travel opportunities
volunteer

Unit 10 Customs
arrange (arrange a surprise party)
celebrate
cheek
comfortable (with)
funeral
gift certificate
impersonal
impolite
memorable
personal
polite
special event
street stall
tip
uncomfortable (with)

Unit 11 Free Time
bungee jumping
comedy club
discount store
fantastic
film festival
fitness center
hang out
hot spot
inexpensive
magic show
reasonable
recommend
(go) surfing
surf the Internet
take-out food
tasty

Unit 12 Movies
actor
actress
animated movie
civilization
comedy
depressing
drama
escape
funny
gangster
jungle
moving
nuclear bomb
prisoner
romance
sci-fi movie
smoke signal
special effects
uplifting
worth (worth seeing)

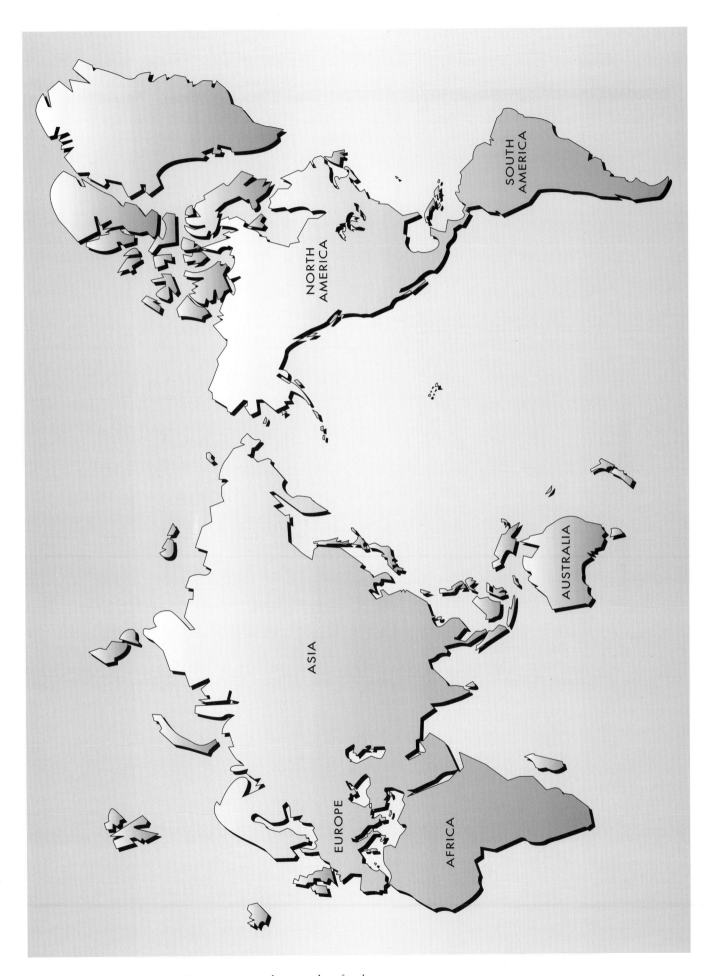

NOTES